PRAISE FOR *THE RETAIL START-UP BOOK*

'Retail is detail! If I had had the benefit of reading this book before I opened my first shop in The Royal Exchange, it would have been plain sailing.'
Simon Crowther, Senior Executive in the retail, clothing and manufacturing industry

'There are many grey areas in business along with the noise created by excessive information that doesn't address the real issues. *The Retail Start-Up Book* provides practical, up-to-date information from seasoned businessmen. It's an invaluable resource for anyone starting a business.'
Toks Aruoture, Founder, The Baby Cot Shop

'When we first introduced the Hugo Boss brand to the UK, Rowland Gee fully understood the brand philosophy and its potential. Our unique marketing strategy, as well as the advanced styling and use of new materials, were warmly welcomed by the Cecil Gee clientele. This led to the eventual development of Hugo Boss standalone shops which were managed and run successfully by Rowland's company without ever compromising the ethos of the brand. This book highlights his wealth of experience and his expertise in retail.'
Detlef Doerge, former Managing Director, Hugo Boss UK

'Rowland was and still is one of the most passionate retailers on the UK high street. His energy has always stood out, as have his taste levels. He always taught those around him to have a can-do attitude in all circumstances, and *The Retail Start-Up Book* is a manifestation both of his enthusiasm and the generosity with which he offers guidance to new businesses.'
Simon Berwin, former Managing Director, Berwin & Berwin Ltd

'Rowland Gee came on board at Me and Maya as a consultant for a year in 2016 to help streamline the business and steer it in the right direction. His help was invaluable in making me realize the brand had a market and that I should pursue selling online. This book brings much of that advice into one resource.'

Lalita Russell-Smith, Founder, Me and Maya

The Retail Start-Up Book

Successfully plan, launch
and grow a business

Rowland Gee
Danny Sloan
Graham Symes

KoganPage

First published in Great Britain and the United States in 2019 by Kogan Page Limited

2nd Floor, 45 Gee Street
London
EC1V 3RS
United Kingdom

122 W 27th St, 10th Floor
New York, NY 10001
USA

4737/23 Ansari Road
Daryaganj
New Delhi 110002
India

www.koganpage.com

© Rowland Gee, Danny Sloan and Graham Symes, 2019

The right of Rowland Gee, Danny Sloan and Graham Symes to be identified as the authors of this work has been asserted by them in accordance with the Copyright, Designs and Patents Act 1988.

ISBNs

Hardback   978 0 7494 9875 7
Paperback   978 0 7494 8472 9
Ebook   978 0 7494 8473 6

British Library Cataloguing-in-Publication Data

A CIP record for this book is available from the British Library.

Library of Congress Cataloging-in-Publication Data

Names: Gee, Rowland, author.
Title: The retail start-up book : successfully plan, launch and grow a
  business / Rowland Gee, Danny Sloan, Graham Symes.
Description: 1 Edition. | New York : Kogan Page Ltd, [2019]
Identifiers: LCCN 2019006377| ISBN 9780749484729 (pbk.) | ISBN 9780749498757
  (hardback) | ISBN 9780749484736 (eISBN)
Subjects: LCSH: Stores, Retail. | New business enterprises. | Strategic
  planning.
Classification: LCC HF5429 .G364 2019 | DDC 658.8/7–dc23 LC record available at
  https://lccn.loc.gov/2019006377

Typeset by Integra Software Services, Pondicherry
Print production managed by Jellyfish
Printed and bound by Ashford Colour Press Ltd.

CONTENTS

Introduction

You will be aware that retail is going through seismic changes. But, interestingly, the 'retail cake' has not shrunk, meaning that the amount of money we spend in the shops and online has not diminished. In fact, over the past five years, money spent in the UK (in shops and online) has grown by 13 per cent and continues to accelerate. In cash terms, £68 billion is now spent online in the UK, accounting for just under 20 per cent of all retail sales, excluding fuel. In the USA, the percentage spent online is rising fast and is forecast to reach 14 per cent by 2021. Similar growth is being seen in Australia, Canada and across the European Union. In Germany, one-eighth of the total retail spend is now spent online, equating to 58 billion euros.

It is how and where we spend that is dramatically changing. There are big winners and big losers. Retailers who have not confronted the changing ways in which people shop, and the products and services demanded, have been shocked by how fast their fortunes have declined, and conversely those who have recognized the behavioural changes have prospered.

This book will help you to understand these changing patterns and to navigate a successful path. A retail career can be very rewarding emotionally as well as financially because you are able to measure – very quickly – the satisfaction the product you choose and the experience you offer has with the customer.

We offer you a solutions-focused book. Throughout, we will explain ways for you to plan, grow and survive in the retail space and how best to become a winner. We've found many other resources that are impractical, which offer solutions that in many cases are impossible to act on. They can also be prone to exaggeration and over-simplistic explanations.

Being a good retailer is not good enough today. Being exceptional or even sensational must be the target start-up retailers set themselves. The most successful retail start-up founders are hardworking individuals, focused and dedicated to delivering their vision. They don't idealize the start-up lifestyle: they have to lead, be prepared to multi-task and quickly understand that if they don't do it, no one else will. It takes a special kind of dedication and unwavering tenacity to make it work.

Retail giant Amazon was once a start-up. In an interview with *The Times*, founder Jeff Bezos warns that to have a vision while not being prepared to constantly accept change can be fatal for retailers. 'The one thing I know about customers is that they are divinely discontent,' he said. 'Expectations are never static, they always go up. People always want better and yesterday's wow quickly becomes today's ordinary.' He also stressed that 'customers will never allow you to rest on your laurels'.

It's how you think about achieving your vision; and it is taking the 'long lens' approach that will set you apart. To succeed, you must know your market, be relentlessly curious, carefully target the customer you want to attract, communicate your product clearly, control and understand your business and, of course, manage your money. Scary headlines like 'high street dying', 'no point competing with Amazon' and 'customers not spending' are examples of what must not be allowed to affect your thought processes.

Because, despite the upheaval the retail industry is experiencing, an abundance of growth opportunities across a diverse range of retail sectors, both in the UK and in international markets, continues to exist. More than ever before, retail consumers focus on individual company propositions and expect to access these retailers in many ways. Early stage retailers that integrate online and physical stores, and that recognize the demands of today's consumer, will enjoy significant upside potential. If you open a physical shop, it is highly likely it will be in a small- to medium-sized town where the local authority will be active and interested.

Starting a business today is an opportunity, and there are many exceptional examples of how to think in a fresh and innovative way to challenge the doomsayers and make your mark. This book provides examples and case studies of what good looks like and will reveal how those people behind the stories achieved their successes. It will clearly explain why retailing is worth pursuing as a start-up business – and, with our help, you will have the best chance of making a success of your unique enterprise.

So, finally, thank you for selecting this book. We hope you enjoy reading it and that it helps you to realize both your dreams and your business objectives in the world of retail.

References and useful resources

References

Low, V (1 May 2018) 'Quiet please! Amazon meetings begin in silence', *The Times* [online]. Available at: https://www.thetimes.co.uk/article/quiet-please-amazon-meetings-begin-in-silence-wd0zmhzc0

Statista (2019) 'Retail e-commerce sales in the United States from 2017 to 2023 (in million U.S. dollars)' [online]. Available at: https://www.statista.com/statistics/272391/us-retail-e-commerce-sales-forecast/

Website

https://www.ons.gov.uk/

Part One
Getting to Grips with Retail

The issues facing the UK retail trade today

Key points

Financial statistics

The online phenomenon

Start-ups statistics and business size definitions

VAT and the start-up

Point of Consumption (POC) tax

Retail space

Household spending per head

Charity shops

There are many factors to consider in the retail industry today, and in this chapter we will introduce some of the focus points you – as an early stage start-up retailer – should begin to gain a thorough understanding of. Looking first at statistics and trends for start-ups, we will also cover some of the biggest changes in the industry, including the rise of online retailing and what that means for retailers, the changing expectations around leasing arrangements for retailers who are considering opening a physical store, changing spending within the household and why you should be aware that charity shops account for a significant part of the retail landscape. We focus on retail sales that exclude food and fuel, as do our charts, although it should be noted that some of the UK's largest food retailers now stock products other than food. Sales of food, however, accounts for more than 85 per cent of the UK's largest food retailers' turnover.

Financial statistics

In the UK, 10 per cent of the working population, amounting to 3.2 million people, work in the retail industry either online or in bricks-and-mortar stores. Some 10 per cent of the UK's gross domestic product (GDP) is spent on retail. Of the UK's 5.7 million private sector businesses (non-government run), 10 per cent operate in the retail space. That's 570,000 businesses, of which 430,000 (or 76 per cent) are sole traders, half of which are registered for VAT.

Looking at a 12-month analysis of retail sales shows that in 2017 the amount of money spent in the retail industry (excluding fuel) increased by 4.7 per cent to approximately £366 billion, when compared with the previous year's £350 billion. Also in 2017, online-only sales increased at a rapid rate, by 15.9 per cent compared to the growth in sales within stores by 2.3 per cent from the previous year. Despite the stronger online presence, consumers spent most of their money in shops and stores. The majority of online spending was done within non-store retail.

Profits from UK retail business in 2017–18

UK retail business split between large and small businesses, 2017–18

Total cash sales: £366bn

Large businesses: £292bn

Small businesses: £74bn (share 26%)

Food: £179bn | Growth over 5 years | 5.7%

Figure 1.1   12-month analysis (excluding food and fuel) of UK retail sales £bn by sector breakdown, 2018

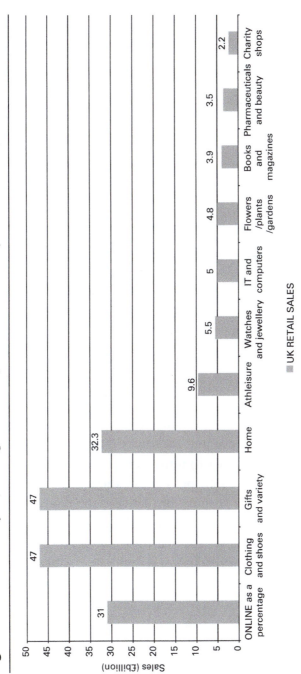

■ UK RETAIL SALES

SOURCE https://www.ons.gov.uk/businessindustryandtrade/retailindustry/bulletins/retailsales/previousReleases

Figure 1.2   Five-year analysis (excluding food and fuel) of UK retail sales £bn by percentage growth

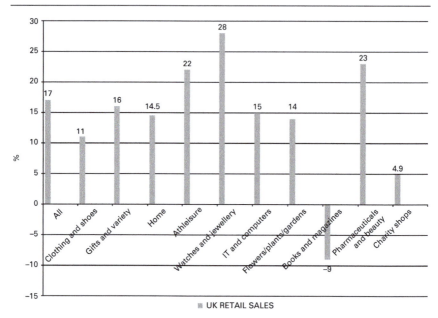

SOURCE https://www.ons.gov.uk/businessindustryandtrade/retailindustry/bulletins/retailsales/previousReleases

Online sales in 2017–18 continued to increase as a proportion of all retail sales, and now account for nearly 20 per cent of all retail sales in the UK, in volume (cash) terms. The small business share of online sales amounted to 53 per cent of these increased sales, which indicates that if the proposition delivers the consumer's expectation, then it is immaterial whether the product originates from a large or small company. The year-on-year increase of 9.4 per cent (https://www.ons.gov.uk) in total online retailing continues the pattern of growth. Non-store retailing is still by far the largest contributor (80 per cent) to the proportion of spending online. Stores with a physical presence continue to increase their online spending (20 per cent), with strong year-on-year growth. Online sales from stores with a physical presence are the largest contributor to the overall growth over the last 12 months.

The online phenomenon

'Retail is being "re-set",' said Virgil Abloh on his appointment in March 2018 as Menswear Artistic Director at Louis Vuitton, a company expanding online as well as in stores.

These are exciting times for retail start-ups, as new technology becomes more accessible and pioneering companies such as Farfetch and Alibaba pave the way. Consumers' online behaviour has radically changed expectations of bricks-and-mortar retailers. Many floundering bricks-and-mortar retailers are struggling precisely because they have failed to adapt to the massive increase in online sales and have neglected to consider how the online experience has changed shoppers' expectations. When people shop online, they make quick decisions based on the following points:

- Is the product easily found by search?
- Is the price clear?
- Are complementary add-ons or alternatives being presented?
- Is a hard-to-find product available?
- Does the site convey the mindset, aesthetic feel and attitude of the shopper?
- When will the item be delivered?
- Is the check-out process efficient and trouble-free?

At the moment it's these key points that, if well delivered, are driving online sales. The answers to them are clear to the shopper in a very short period of time, probably a matter of minutes. If the shopper is satisfied, then the experience will be positive. However, if any of these points fail to be satisfactorily met, it's highly likely the customer will leave the site and, in many cases, never return. In an era of online shopping, loyalty is rare and rapid satisfaction is demanded.

These behavioural patterns are now woven into the minds of the bricks-and-mortar shopper, and so it is also the expectation that this level of service will be replicated on the high street. The shop operator not only has to accept this change, but has to adapt to ensure its level of service matches the best online operators. The physical shop must therefore also have an easily identifiable, carefully selected group of complementary products; it must present and merchandise them in an atmosphere that relates to that shopper's emotions and is consistent with the retail proposition. Features and benefits of a product and the price should be immediately clear, and once the product is selected the check-out process must be swift and properly managed. At the moment, there is significant evidence that many bricks-and-mortar retailers are not getting it – and indeed, the rapid rise of the increasing online spend proves the point (Deloitte, 2017).

This is the opportunity that the start-up has to grasp. First, think like an online operator if you plan to open a shop. Second, ensure that online becomes part of your whole proposition.

Consider Selfridges, a high-end UK department store established in central London by an American, Harry Gordon Selfridge, in 1909. It is an example of a unique and successful enterprise that has never stood still in over a century. The outstanding website sets it apart from the crowd – it is visual, functional and easy to navigate, and it ticks all the boxes for good website design.

Selfridges' website includes:

- punchy home page;
- this week's must-see items highlighted;
- brilliant graphics and photography;
- podcast series up front;
- what's happening in store;
- clear navigation tabs and drop-down menus;
- clear prices and easy check out;
- quick-view technology;
- no time-wasting as stock position is clear and everything on show is in stock;
- fast functions.

Outstanding website design can also be seen in the following brands trading in the UK and around the world. These brands and organizations are worth looking at because they clearly demonstrate best in class.

While these businesses focus on widely different products and services, they all clearly communicate their respective brand visions and remain loyal to the aspirations and expectations of their customers. The factors that link this exceptional group are that they all show clarity of the core product selection and complementary items, perform logistical excellence, retain their demographic focus and adopt appropriate aesthetics.

Examples of best-in-class websites

- Westfield Shopping Centres: https://uk.westfield.com/london
- Tate Gallery London: http://shop.tate.org.uk
- Victoria and Albert Museum London: https://www.vam.ac.uk/shop/
- Cotswold Trading (gift store): https://www.cotswoldtrading.com
- Paul A Young Chocolatier: http://www.paulayoung.co.uk
- Twenty Twenty Gallery (art gallery and gift store): https://www.twenty-twenty.co.uk
- Japan House (cultural centre): https://www.japanhouselondon.uk/the-shop/
- Gandys (clothes and accessories store): http://www.gandyslondon.com/
- Typo (gift store): https://typo.com/UK/
- The Longest Stay (home furnishings store): https://www.thelongeststay.com

---

CASE STUDY   HEMA

The Hollandsche Eenheidsprijzen Maatschappij Amsterdam, or HEMA, opened its first department store in Amsterdam on 4 November 1926. The founders wanted to open a department store that was accessible to everyone. Before this, department stores were very much aimed at wealthy people, and most store personnel spoke only French. Although HEMA remains loyal to its longstanding history, it demonstrates in an outstanding way how it has transformed itself to meet the demands of today's consumer. Each product for sale, either in store or online, is displayed clearly and the company gives a commitment that every one of its products is sourced by and unique to HEMA. It also offers online shopping in all the countries in which it now operates.

For a company founded in 1926, HEMA demonstrates brilliantly the reality of the re-setting of retail. It underlines what we advise you throughout this book: the importance of establishing a 'private label' collection of products, expressing your brand ethos in a positive, witty and assured way, and thus communicating confidence in the products you sell to your customers.

Start-ups statistics and business size definitions

According to figures published by the Centre for Entrepreneurs (CfE) think tank, the number of UK start-ups launched in 2017, across all industries, amounted to 589,000. Consider this in context:

- 589,000 UK business start-ups launched in 2017 in total.
- Just under 60,000 were retail start-ups.

Also in 2017, high streets in the UK saw a 1 per cent drop in vacant units. This is evidence of the increasing measures landlords and city councils are taking to reduce the vacancy rates across their towns by allowing the changing of use of persistently vacant units. Councils are also becoming more willing to invest in the town centres, demonstrated by recent council purchases in Canterbury and Shrewsbury, for example, of commercial and retail property originally owned by companies that went out of business. These purchases enable councils to take full ownership of their town centres and enable them to implement their wider regeneration plans.

The UK's major cities continue to dominate the country's entrepreneurial dynamism. The combined authorities of London lead with 205,325 businesses registered last year, followed by Birmingham with 17,473, Manchester with 9,416, Glasgow with 7,845 and Leeds with 7,645. Edinburgh, Bristol, Liverpool and Brighton also rank among the top 20.

Nevertheless, the following small, medium and large towns, as well as areas of London are seeing net growth in independent retail business start-ups (in alphabetical order):

Aberdeen

Barking Road, London

Barry West

Bethnal Green, London

Blackpool

Brixton, London

Bromborough Rake (near Liverpool)

Conwy, Wales

Dawley

Edinburgh

Erdington

Finsbury Park, London

Folkestone

Goodmayes, London

Gravesend

Great Yarmouth

Liverpool

Ludlow

Malton

Market Harborough

Narborough Road, Leicester

Newcastle upon Tyne

Notting Hill, London

Old Bexley, London

Otley

Paisley

Portobello Road, London

Reddish

Saltley

Scarborough

Southport

Sparkhill

St. Ives, Cornwall

Stoke Newington, London

Teignmouth

Tooting, London

Totnes

Upton Park, London

Walton Street, London

West End, Morecambe

Weymouth

Whitby

Witney

Figure 1.3 The UK net shop openings, by trade, between 2012 and 2017. It also shows net closures by trade in 2017

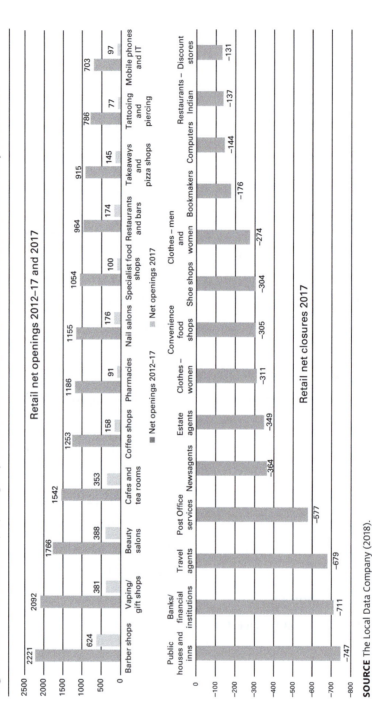

Retail net openings 2012–17 and 2017

Trade	Net openings 2012–17	Net openings 2017
Barber shops	2221	624
Vaping/gift shops	2092	381
Banks/financial institutions	1766	388
Beauty salons	1542	353
Cafes and tea rooms	1253	158
Coffee shops	1186	91
Pharmacies	1155	176
Nail salons	1054	100
Specialist food shops	964	174
Restaurants and bars	915	145
Takeaways and pizza shops	786	77
Tattooing and piercing	703	97
Mobile phones and IT		

Retail net closures 2017

Trade	Net closures 2017
Public houses and inns	–747
Banks/financial institutions	–711
Travel agents	–679
Post Office services	–577
Newsagents	–364
Estate agents	–349
Clothes – women	–311
Convenience food shops	–305
Shoe shops	–304
Clothes – men and women	–274
Bookmakers	–176
Computers	–144
Restaurants – Indian	–137
Discount stores	–131

SOURCE The Local Data Company (2018).

Business size definitions

It's also worth understanding how these start-up businesses can be categorized, and sizes are defined as follows:

- A micro business employs no one apart from the owner.
- A small business employs 1–49 employees.
- A medium-size business employs 50–249 employees.
- A large business employs 250 or more employees.

Interestingly, in the United States, it is not the largest cities that are experiencing retail start-up growth. Smaller cities have worked hard to regenerate their communities by stepping in to offer deals and incentives to new retailers. These are very similar initiatives to those of the UK. Comparable approaches are also taking place in Canada and in Australia, where the big ten shopping destinations are receiving political and financial support for smaller, new entry, retailers.

A good case in point is Australia's thriving coffee culture, which proved to be a challenge for Starbucks. The country has been immersed in the café scene since the mid-1900s when Italian and Greek immigrants moved to the continent. Because the Australian consumer had become used to espresso coffee and the coffee shops refused to dilute its offer, the consumer stayed loyal and the government backed local industry.

VAT and the start-up

A little-known fact in the UK is that even if your sales are below the VAT threshold (£85k as of 2018) and you are therefore not required to pay VAT on your sales, you can still recover the VAT you pay on products or services you receive.

Point of Consumption (POC) tax

In the United States, some states have gained the right to charge tax (typically about 6 per cent) on e-commerce sales where no physical store exists. Online retailers have so far been exempt from sales tax in the USA and from business rates in the UK. This may well change as governments all over the world are being challenged to create a fairer local tax collection system that does not discriminate against rent- and UK business rate-paying, physical operations.

Amazon has already begun to collect tax on its own web sales in 45 US states, anticipating a change that will in due course affect on-line retailers.

Tip

If you plan to be an online retailer only or a third-party seller, for example on Amazon, factor into your margin a low single digit percentage on your cost price that might cover a new point of consumption tax on online retailers. A third-party seller selling through Amazon pays the company about 18 per cent on its sales or revenues. This percentage includes storage and dispatch. As a third-party seller, it's important to be prepared for this extra POC tax – but don't be too hasty in moving away from Amazon. It is expected that Amazon will soon announce a service to mitigate this to keep you loyal. If you do move away, keep in mind that given the knowledge of your sales, Amazon may be in a position to 'mop up' those sales with another product.

Retail space

As we've already made clear so far in this book, the retail industry is going through a very big change. To quote Virgil Abloh again, 'There's a new establishment happening and it's time to be assertive' (2018).

The Royal Institution of Chartered Surveyors (RICS) states that rental expectations for physical shops are falling sharply, landlord in-ducements are increasing and space is available. As a consequence of these changes, landlords are having to reduce the capital value of their properties and are offering financial inducements to incoming tenants to avoid empty shop rates. So, not only are rents being lowered, but landlords are open to both short leases and licences. Historically, a lease (under the most recent Landlord and Tenant Act 1987) is a legally binding, secure tenure contract binding on both parties and usually extends to ten years with an upward-only review after five years. This arrangement is now being challenged and landlords are beginning to realize that occupiers no longer want this 'ball and chain' commitment. The licence, on the other hand, gives the occupier a shorter-term agreement with a much greater degree of flexibility, albeit less security in that the landlord can terminate the licence at the end of the mutually agreed term. This arrangement allows the occupier to test the viability of the proposition and also removes from the landlord the statutory obligation to pay empty shop rates.

A recent paper from the Centre for Cities, reported in *The Times* by Philip Aldrick on 26 June 2018, criticized many local authorities for not allowing unoccupied shops to be turned into homes. Some authorities have permitted this change of use and this has helped some local high streets become places where communities can 'live, work, shop and play'.

CASE STUDY   Appear Here

In 2013, Ross Bailey launched Appear Here, an online marketplace for short-term retail spaces that matchmakes landlords with tenants. Appear Here is a disrupter; it's simply a great innovation for start-ups and there is no one else with a database that comes close. As Natalie Massenet, founder of designer fashion portal Net-a-Porter, said in the *Financial Times* on 29 July 2018, 'it's good for brands because they don't have to commit to long leases and big upfront fitouts'.

We like Appear Here because their reach is impressive – they operate in London, Paris and New York, and they represent every type of retail business. They also offer a collection of modular furniture suitable for small shops and short-term lets that can be rented by the week. In the same *Financial Times* article, Ross Bailey is bullish about the high street, but is clear that it must adapt. As he says, 'Your shop doesn't need to be in one place anymore… before, if you didn't have a shop your business was over because people couldn't find you… now with online you've always got presence.' We also agree with him when he says, 'Digital, direct-to-consumer brands are paying so much for digital advertising that they're finding that a physical store is a better way to communicate with customers. One little shop can create something that can build a connection with millions of people who never walk by.' Bailey's hope is that the pop-up will restore life and fun to the high street again and make it a place of discovery. Just make sure when they discover you, they never forget you.

Tip

If you choose to open a physical shop, look for areas where councils and local authorities have adopted a progressive approach and welcome pop-ups.

Household spending per head

In the UK, the largest sections of the population are represented in the age groups 25–40 and 50–65. The median age of males is 40, while for females it is 42. In the next 20 years, the population in the UK is expected to grow by 9 per cent.

In 2017, UK households showed current price spending per head grew by £589 compared with 2016, an increase of 3.1 per cent. This is encouraging for start-up retailers. In current price terms, seasonally adjusted, retail consumer spending in Quarter 4 (Oct to Dec) 2017 has now reached £4,890 per head. This is an increase of £36 (0.7 per cent) per head when compared with Quarter 3 (July to Sept) 2017. In volume terms, there has been an increase of 0.1 per cent per head, indicating that consumers spent more because they bought more units (volume statistics) in addition to the effect of increasing prices. This is good because it demonstrates that inflation is very much under control in the UK. The ONS provides data on both volume (units) and value (cash) for every segment in the retail market. Total per-head spending has now reached £19,394 in 2017, with housing and transport making the largest contributions of £5,153 and £2,528 respectively. The third-largest contribution to overall per-head spending can be seen in miscellaneous, where spending in 2017 reached £2,499. Comparing spending by types of goods and services (in current price terms), households have continued to spend most on services. In 2017, spending on services – which includes spending on essential items such as housing and transport – grew to its highest level since the start of these reports, and is now at £11,214, contributing 58.3 per cent of total household spending.

Population statistics

66.5m (UK)

326m (USA)

82.3m (Germany)

65.2m (France)

In the UK, the percentage of consumer spending per capita exceeds America by 39 per cent, Germany by 25 per cent and France by 25 per cent.

Charity shops

The 26th annual Charity Shops Survey 2017–18 collected data from 76 charities operating 6,722 shops, with a combined income of more than £863m (which accounts for 5 per cent of the UK's non-food retail sales 2017–18). The figures cover charities' most recent financial years at the time of the data collection, which for most respondents was the 12 months leading to March 2018.

The Top Ten

1 British Heart Foundation, income: £176.4m, shops: 724

2 Oxfam GB, income: £92.5m, shops: 640

3 Cancer Research UK, income: £84.5m, shops: 594

4 Barnardo's, income: £70.3m, shops: 710

5 Sue Ryder, income: £55.0m, shops: 451

6 Salvation Army, income: £48.0m, shops: 230

7 Age UK, income: £42.6m, shops: 404

8 British Red Cross, income: £30.0m, shops: 341

9 Scope, income: £21.3m, shops: 225

10 Marie Curie, income: £16.4m, shops: 178

The 26th annual survey indicated that, for the first time in 14 years, there were no more openings of charity shops than were closed. The reason is partly related to tougher high street conditions in recent years and partly because costs have risen by 4.1 per cent, principally caused by the 4.7 per cent increase in staff costs (pushed up by the introduction of the National Living Wage in April 2016) coupled with a reduction in volunteer numbers. Consequently, charity shop profits have fallen for the second year running.

It's worth being aware of these movements, as charity shops account for significant competition to many small shops because they are allowed to purchase new merchandise and because they are able to work on much lower margins than traditional retailers since they do not pay business rates.

References and useful resources

References and further reading

Centre for Entrepreneurs (16 Jan 2017) '2016 breaks business formation records' [online]. Available at: https://centreforentrepreneurs.org/cfe-releases/2016-breaks-business-formation-records/

Creevy, J (5 Oct 2010) 'Tesco non-food sales grow to £6.5bn', *Drapers* [online]. Available at: https://www.drapersonline.com/retail/multiples/tesco-non-food-sales-grow-to-65bn/5017877.article

Forbes (13 Dec 2010) 'America's 25 Best Cities For Shopping' [online]. Available at: https://www.forbes.com/2010/12/13/best-cities-for-shopping-forbes-woman-time-retail-walmart-sales-tax_slide.html

Hopkinson, M (3 July 2013) 'The Grimsey Review 2 (2018)', Didobi [online]. Available at: https://www.didobi.com/the-grimsey-review/

Klara, R (11 Nov 2017) 'Bad news, brick-and-mortar stores: the internet finally has you beat', *AdWeek* [online]. Available online at: https://www.adweek.com/brand-marketing/bad-news-brick-and-mortar-stores-the-internet-finally-has-you-beat/

National Statistics (30 Nov 2017), Business population estimates 2017 [online]. Available at: https://www.gov.uk/government/statistics/business-population-estimates-2017

Preston, R (2 Oct 2017) 'UK's largest charity shop retailers revealed in survey', Civil Society [online]. Available at: https://www.civilsociety.co.uk/news/uks-largest-charity-retailers-revealed-in-league-table.html

Turner, A (25 July 2018) 'Why there are almost no Starbucks in Australia', CNBC [online]. Available at: https://www.cnbc.com/2018/07/20/starbucks-australia-coffee-failure.html

WWD (26 March 2018) 'Louis Vuitton Hires Virgil Abloh to Heat Up Men's' [online]. Available at: https://wwd.com/fashion-news/designer-luxury/louis-vuitton-virgil-abloh-menswear-artistic-director-exclusive-1202638255/

Websites

https://centreforentrepreneurs.org/
https://www.ft.com
https://www.hemashop.com/gb/

Useful resources

https://www.localdatacompany.com/
https://www.ons.gov.uk/
https://www.ons.gov.uk/businessindustryandtrade/retailindustry/bulletins/retailsales/previousReleases

https://www.ons.gov.uk/economy/nationalaccounts/satelliteaccounts/
bulletins/consumertrends/octobertodecember2017#household-spending-
per-head

https://www.rics.org/uk/knowledge/market-analysis/rics-uk-commercial-
market-survey/

https://www.statista.com/topics/831/per-capita-expenditure/

https://tradingeconomics.com/united-kingdom/consumer-spending

http://www.worldometers.info/world-population/population-by-country/

http://worldpopulationreview.com/countries/united-kingdom-population/

Part Two
Creating Your Retail Marketing Plan

Analysing and positioning your retail business in the existing market

02

Key points

Understand the market you'll be working in

Work out your 'place' in the market

Always reflect on how your product or service is unique

Understand the market

Successful retailers understand in detail the market in which they operate and their competitors. They know the major products and markets that are likely to be able to provide opportunities suitable for their business and they monitor how these are changing. In this, detail is paramount.

The award-winning chef and restaurateur Yotam Ottolenghi reiterates the importance of detail, stating 'Tweak and tweak until the details are right. It's about having the energy of the long-distance runner and the sprinter' (O'Hara, 2015). This focus is important, as is the wisdom to listen when the details don't go to plan and then changing them.

Your place in the market

Retail marketing is an important aspect of doing business and should be given the same status to any other business function. It can best be described simply as identifying who your target customers are, understanding what they want and satisfying their needs in a way that will deliver what you are trying to achieve for your retail business: profitability, survival or growth.

The key is to develop a sense of your high-level 'mission statement' or purpose and keep this simple and practical. You need to know what function your business is going to serve as well as have a broad view of your overall plan. Ask yourself what major things you are planning to do and what aspects of establishing your business will have an impact on that plan.

Key steps

Research

As a first step, develop and finalize your research brief by defining what you are trying to achieve. This should include your objectives, timing and budgets; you should also set aside time to evaluate results. There are several key areas to constructing your brief. As already stated, it's essential to really understand and know your own business and the marketplace in which you operate.

If you are already selling your product, ask how you compare to the competition. Research pricing – consider what your pricing policy is, and how your position compares with your competitors. The research outputs will help you to compile a list of actions you need to take to achieve and maintain a competitive edge. As a start-up, the cost of conducting any market research does not need to be vastly expensive, but it is an important consideration.

There are two types of research: primary and secondary. Primary, or field research, involves interviews and surveys, observations and experiments, and is carried out for a specific purpose. Secondary, or desktop, involves reviewing research and data that already exists and can be accessed via available channels, for example, online reports.

The results you record in your research can be either qualitative (this is what people think; it is subjective and open to interpretation) or quantitative (this involves hard facts and statistics eg volume sales figures).

Once you have established your brief, we would suggest using a combination of both research approaches. In the early stages, this will keep the costs to a minimum. However, you and your team do need to put time and energy into doing most of the ground work. As well as time spent conducting the research, make sure you also consider the time needed for planning and preparation of the questions you want to ask or the experiments you want to undertake, and allow sufficient post-research time to evaluate your results.

The timing of your research is another factor to consider. Research can and should be carried out at different times of the year and should be carried out before and immediately after your start-up period.

Competition

Ask yourself systematically what products you're selling, what their market position is and what competition you face for those products. New competitors are entering and exiting the marketplace frequently. This, combined with changes in customer behaviours, means that keeping up to date with these changes are key to maintaining your competitive advantage. Jack Welch, the former CEO of General Electric, said 'An organizational ability to learn and translate that learning into action rapidly is the ultimate competitive advantage' (Stack, 2013). Competition examples in the retail industry often focus around the big supermarkets, or on the online retailers versus the independents. It is true that many small-town shopping areas have declined as a result of the changing retail climate. However, it is also true that where independent retailers work closely with local councils and others including landlords they have fought back to create competitive shopping experiences. Investment in the town centre experience – attracting unique independents to complement the overall retail mix – delivers a very powerful retail concept. Combine this with frequent experiential marketing events, seasonal markets, car shows, fairs, music and beer festivals, and it's possible to keep the retail spirit alive and kicking.

Differentiate

Differentiation is simply defined as standing out from the crowd to attract and retain customers. Focus your efforts on how your product or service offering will be better than, or different from, what is already available to customers. There are several areas to explore that can help you to achieve this.

It's important to learn how to build a positive reputation for service and reliability. This can only be done over time and relies on you to deliver consistency in everything you do. Convenience is another big differentiator – make it easy for your customers to shop with you, whether this is instore or online. You can also consider selling unique products by origin, special packaging, size or branding. Sell not just by price (high or low), but create real value. Over time, this will create powerful customer loyalty and help you not only to retain customers but also to attract new ones.

Customer service delivery

In our opinion, true customer service delivery levels should be measured when things go wrong, not when things are going smoothly. You and your employees need to step up when things go wrong, because customers will measure you on how well you respond. Examples of poor service range from a customer waiting a long period at check out, while noticing two or three or more unattended tills at peak periods, to having a poor customer returns policy that is defensive and difficult, or running out of stock – which is not only bad service, but costly to your business in terms of a sale you would have otherwise made.

Ensuring you have good, empowered instore management who can anticipate problems and deliver solutions will prove invaluable. If your business relies on people to deliver or provide a service, ensure you recruit the right people in terms of quality and experience. Write all processes down, and ensure proper time is allocated for training to ensure consistent delivery of service. Many sales organizations have recognized this link between training and sales, and the return on investment can deliver substantial growth.

> **Tip**
>
> Remember the people who you employ are your ambassadors. They need to understand your unique brand message to be able to convey that to potential customers. On the front line, they will be delivering the first and last messages to your customers.

CASE STUDY   Dyson

A new product was in the making in 1978, when James Dyson became frustrated with his vacuum cleaner's diminishing performance over time and resolved to uncover the reason. He took it apart and discovered that its bag was clogging with dust, causing suction to drop. Taking inspiration from an industrial cyclone tower he built at his factory, which separated paint particles from the air using outward-moving force, he realized the same principle could be applied to a household vacuum. Five years and 5,127 prototypes later, he had invented the world's first bagless vacuum cleaner. Now, Dyson is a brand name known worldwide – and present in households in 75 countries around the world (dyson.com.au).

Dyson clearly demonstrates how constant refining and development of his idea coupled with a great deal of perseverance led to success. His philosophy on learning by failure is best summed up by his statement, 'Failure is interesting – it's part of making progress. You never learn from success, but you do learn from failure' (Goodman, 2012).

Dyson has grown from one man and one idea to a technology company with over 1,000 engineers worldwide. And it doesn't stand still. At its core is an ever-growing team of engineers and scientists; more ideas mean more invention. Dyson products have gained a distinct reputation for their quality, ergonomics and contemporary design, and have become one of the UK's most desirable products.

Their appliances are offered in a range of different shapes, sizes and colours to meet the demands of their target markets, and Dyson then further enhances its range by offering a great after-sales service. Expert customer service is available seven days a week, and step-by-step tools for trouble-shooting help you to get your machine working. Online support includes how-to videos, helpful tips and free Dyson parts and labour during the guarantee period. If your machine can't be repaired whilst under guarantee they have a hassle-free replacement policy in place. Even after the guarantee has expired, Dyson will still be on hand to help. In the customer care call centre, unlike traditional call centres where representatives are tethered to their phones and computers and are often reading a script from a screen, Dyson staff wear wireless headsets so they can walk over to stations that house current and past models of the company's products. Representatives often go through the same steps of taking apart a vacuum cleaner as they give customers trouble-shooting steps.

Dyson provides an excellent example of refining a product, and then continuing to evolve to meet the needs of the customer and the market, refining the details and improving at every step.

References and useful resources

Dyson.com.au (2018) 'Meet James Dyson – The Inventor of Cyclonic Vacuum' [online]. Available at: https://www.dyson.com.au/community/about-james-dyson.aspx [Accessed 2 June 2018].

Dyson.co.uk (2018) 'Get Expert Help from Dyson Support' [online]. Available at: https://www.dyson.co.uk/support/journey/overview.html

Goodman, N (2012) 'James Dyson on Using Failure to Drive Success' [online] *Entrepreneur*. Available at: https://www.entrepreneur.com/article/224855

O'Hara, G (2015) Defining the entrepreneur [online] Kinfolk. Available at: https://kinfolk.com/defining-the-entrepreneur/

Stack, L (2013) The ultimate competitive advantage: translating learning into action, Theproductivitypro.com [online]. Available at: http://theproductivitypro.com/blog/2013/08/the-ultimate-competitive-advantage-translating-learning-into-action/

Generating a powerful SWOT analysis for your retail business

03

Key points

Be aware of changes in your retail marketplace and be ready to respond

Analyse your strengths and weaknesses

Embrace your opportunities and threats

Self-analysis

SWOT refers to the strengths, weaknesses, opportunities and threats of your retail business. It is a useful analysis tool to specify the objective of your retail business start-up and to identify the internal and external factors that are favourable and unfavourable to achieve that objective.

This simple acronym will help you to work systematically through ways your business is likely to succeed and risks that may cause you problems. Even in the first flush of enthusiasm for your new start-up, you must always be aware of and face up to any awkward truths about your business and be realistic in your expectations.

The SWOT analysis is expanded below, split into two sections: the first looking at your strengths and weaknesses, the second at your opportunities and threats. Use these questions and ideas to closely examine your business idea or existing business and keep a written record of your conclusions. Anticipating how your business may succeed, as well as what may hinder your success, means you can act, rather than react, as your business develops and grows.

Once it's completed, you can use your SWOT analysis to write a statement identifying the key issues you face and detail the opportunities you wish to exploit. Remember, while it's good to identify a wide range of opportunities, make sure you also prioritize which are the most important for your business or the most achievable to begin acting upon. Quality not quantity is key.

Strengths and weaknesses

To begin identifying your business's strengths and weaknesses, start by asking the following questions:

- Do you have a distinctive product or business?
- Do you have distinctive company strengths?
- What is the financial position of the business?
- What is the level of service you provide? Look both at what you think service is like, as well as what customers are telling you – the two may be different!
- What's your client base?
- How do you manage client relationships?
- What is your price or fee structure? Are you aiming to be high, mid, or low in your price point?
- How does this compare with your competitors?
- Who are your distributors or supply chain? Do you use just one or multiple distributors/suppliers? Are they all offering good value?
- What are your promotion and selling tactics?
- Are you aware of any areas of your business that require improvement?

- Are you lacking skills or new products?
- Do you have a higher cost base or lower productivity than your competitors?

Opportunities and threats

- What are you doing to keep up to date with changes in technology and markets?
- Are there any changes in government policy or legislation that will affect your business either now or in the future?
- What local, national and global events may have an impact on your business?
- Are there any potential new uses of products or services you offer?
- What use can you make of marketing or promotional techniques?
- What social factors such as population fluctuation of lifestyle changes may impact your business?

Tip

When considering threats, remember that they can be external or internal – they can be anything that can adversely affect your business. External threats could be inflation, new legislation, or a new competitor in your market. Internal threats could include a skill or staff shortage within your business.

Figure 3.1 An example of a SWOT analysis

Strengths	Weaknesses	Opportunities	Threats
• Location • Management • Employees • Product quality • Service delivery • Exclusive rights • High demand • Existing client base	• Competition • Low margin • High recruitment costs • Supply chain • New entrants to market	• Expanding market • Timing of launch • First to market • Product extensions • Multi-channel • Investment partners • Export market	• Inconsistent supply • Property redevelopment proposals • Inflated rents • Taxation

Competitor analysis

As part of your research into your competitors, it's a good idea to carry out a mini SWOT analysis on each of them. Start by writing a summary of your major competitors. You need to try to forecast where you think they will be during the period of your plan and assess their likely strategies, customers and markets. This in-depth knowledge of your competition and seeing things from their perspective will give you valuable insight.

As a retailer one of your priorities is to work out where your competitors are succeeding, and why. The main question to answer is this: What are they doing to attract more customers than you?

To answer this question, put yourself in the shoes of a customer. Take some time out of your day and get to know your competitors by visiting some of their outlets. Approach it like a mystery shopping experience; think about each of the customer touch points as well as the overall customer experience. Keep the process simple – do not try to capture all the information at the first visit and definitely avoid clipboards and other props.

The purpose of the exercise is to 'act and think like a customer'. You may also want to consider repeating this exercise at different times of the day and months of the year as the results will vary. Take advantage while doing this work to build relationships with potential future customers within the community. Local people are usually only too willing to stop and answer your questions or share their opinions about the local shopping community – they have a wealth of knowledge built up over many years. As an article in Kinfolk on community entrepreneurs observes, 'Neighbourhood shops don't just provide goods and services. They can also become valuable support structures within creative communities.'

Not only will you enjoy this learning experience, but it will generate new profitable ideas and help you to build your knowledge about your competitors. Using your research findings, you should now be able to develop concepts that will help you to join, or beat, the competition. The threats the competition faces are the same threats that you will come to face as well. In that sense, you have common ground.

CASE STUDY   Nestlé – perfect store, perfect journey

What does a confectionery giant have in common with small start-up businesses? How can start-ups learn the conversion process – to turn potential shoppers into profitable buying customers?

Nestlé International Travel Retail have, for many years, led the way in research into the shopping patterns of potential travel retail customers and used these findings to understand how to convert more travellers to shoppers. Nestlé's objectives were to deliver against three common goals that all retailers large or small should aspire to:

- increase footfall in the store space;
- convert shoppers into buyers:
- increase basket size and spend for each transaction.

Nestlé recognized the importance of connecting and engaging with global travellers at different touch points in their journey process. After years of extensive shopper and consumer research, the company developed what it called 'The Perfect Store' concept to help increase customers' spend on confectionery in travel retail stores across Europe. Nestlé achieved their vision and created The Perfect Store through several different steps. First, they made confectionery easier to understand and easier to shop for by displaying it by brand and manufacturer or based on shopper purchase decisions ('Gifts for Him', 'Gifts for Her', 'Family Gifting', etc.). They also encouraged shoppers to engage with their products through the creative, interactive use of fixtures, including points where shoppers could sample chocolates and were played the sounds of Switzerland upon contact. This approach was based on Nestlé research, which had found that 52 per cent of all shoppers who interacted went on to make a purchase. The company made confectionery accessible to all shoppers with the introduction of products at till points where Nestlé research found that impulse buying achieved a 50 per cent rate of sales increase. In addition, small touches like providing ready-to-go gift solutions (with gift bags) proved highly successful. Their strategy also included creating layouts and product positioning based on how shoppers shop and they maintained consistency through the disciplined use of planograms (a visual diagram showing the placement of every product in the store). Finally, Nestlé brought the confectionery category to life by creating bigger, bolder seasonal events, optimizing calendar occasions such as Ramadan, Christmas and Easter.

In 2015, Nestlé announced the launch of 'The Perfect Journey', an evolution of its Perfect Store initiative. The Perfect Journey is an innovative, digital category advice platform and a first for both the confectionery category and the travel retail industry. The platform helps retailers to find the best ways to tailor their existing offering to specific customer profiles.

References and useful resources

Jerven, T and King, GB (2015) 'The Community Entrepreneurs: The Store Owners', Kinfolk [online]. Available at: https://kinfolk.com/the-community-entrepreneurs-the-store-owners/

Ng, M (2009) 'Nestlé drives purchases with "perfect store" concept', *The Moodie Davitt Report* [online]. Available at: https://www.moodiedavittreport.com/nestle-drives-purchases-with-perfect-store-concept-091109/

Planning your retail marketing strategy

Assumptions

It's impossible to predict every trend, movement, competitive action or economic factor in the marketplace but your assumptions, predictions and forecasts should be based on what you know today – so make sure you're keeping a record.

The important point to remember is to not wait too long in creating or continually reviewing the perfect plan – it rarely exists and chances are you will miss the opportunity to get a head start on your competitors in the meantime. Consumer trends develop, information is released and new products are launched every day, so retailers who can be flexible with their plans, build on their knowledge and adapt to their customers' needs are more likely to be a success.

It is far more important to start executing your plan and continue to monitor your assumptions along the way, taking note of any indication of major changes that are a sign it's time to rewrite the plan.

Steve Jobs, co-founder of Apple, said, 'You can't just ask customers what they want and then try and give it to them. By the time you get it built, they'll want something new.' So, aim to become a flexible, agile retailer; one who embraces change and not one who tries to resist it.

Objectives

When you're drafting your plan for your business, always be realistic about what you want to achieve and what your objectives are. Ask yourself:

- Are the objectives clear and to the point?
- Does your team understand them?
- Are they relevant to the business?
- Are they practical and achievable?
- Is the timescale realistic?
- Are you aiming to target existing customers or seeking new business from new customers?
- Are you targeting new revenue from online channels?
- How will you quantify what you are trying to achieve?

The precise direction you want to see your business taking will have an impact on all aspects of your planning and you should keep referring back to your objectives, making sure that all your plans are driving in that direction.

Creating your overall strategy statement

Your overall strategy statement should outline exactly, and clearly, what your brand exists to do and how it does it. It should capture your goals and objectives, and the essence of your business, but also be short and to the point – an elevator pitch for your business, so to speak. To get started, it can be helpful to look at examples of global brands whose products and services exhibit a clear mission statement and where the brand strategy is clearly executed across all facets of the business.

For example, Ben & Jerry's Ice Cream company has a three-part mission statement, divided into Product, Economic and Social, which guides their decision-making. Their product mission drives the team to (most importantly) make great ice cream: 'To make, distribute and sell the finest quality ice cream and euphoric concoctions with a continued commitment to incorporating wholesome, natural ingredients and promoting business practices that respect the Earth and the Environment.'

The economic mission relates to how the company is managed for sustainable financial growth: 'To operate the Company on a sustainable financial basis of profitable growth, increasing value for our stakeholders and expanding opportunities for development and career growth for our employees.'

And finally, the social mission focuses on generating new and innovative ideas to ensure Ben & Jerry's is a company that strives to make the world a better place: 'To operate the Company in a way that actively recognizes the central role that business plays in society by initiating innovative ways to improve the quality of life locally, nationally and internationally' (https://www.benjerry.co.uk/values).

In the world of tourism and hospitality, the Ritz-Carlton Hotel Company has a mission statement that's clear and carried out by their staff across the world. Also referred to as The Credo, it states: 'The Ritz-Carlton is a place where the genuine care and comfort of our guests is our highest mission. We pledge to provide the finest personal service and facilities for our guests who will always enjoy a warm, relaxed, yet refined ambience' (http://www.ritzcarlton.com/en/about/gold-standards).

In the automotive industry, renowned disruptor and innovative brand Tesla's mission statement was: 'To accelerate the world's transition to sustainable transport.' However, in mid-2016, under Elon Musk's leadership, the company changed the corporate mission to 'To accelerate the world's transition to sustainable energy' (https://www.tesla.com/en_GB/about).

When compiling *your* statement you should aim to keep it simple, make it clear and easily understood by customers and staff. Before finalizing your statement, test your ideas and thoughts with people you know and your staff. Listen carefully to their feedback and be prepared to incorporate changes.

Start planning your retail marketing strategy

Drawing on your SWOT analysis (outlined in Chapter 3) and your statement of key issues and opportunities, you should now be able to select the markets in which you want to compete.

Within the markets you've selected, decide how to position your business against your identified competition. External factors will, to some extent, set your objectives in terms of sales and product development.

The aim of your retail marketing plan is to develop strategies to meet those objectives. For a small start-up business, the markets you decide to operate in are key, as realistically you can only operate in a limited number of markets without trying to do more than possible and most likely failing in at least some of them.

Time spent planning which markets will suit you is well spent as you are more likely to achieve success if you have considered the markets thoroughly. Considering the following questions will help you to create a market forecast and to develop a statement describing your approach to your retail market and how you intend to be seen.

Checklist

Market forecast

✓ Who are your customers?

✓ Is there a market niche?

✓ Are customers in this market satisfied or are they looking for something new?

✓ Can you offer them something that really meets their needs?

✓ Will you generate enough business in this market to survive?

✓ Alternatively, is there too much business? Will you overreach yourself?

✓ How will competitors react?

✓ Can you communicate to this market effectively?

Developing an approach statement

✓ Do you have a clear understanding of your customers' needs?

✓ Do you understand your strengths?

✓ How will you differentiate your product/service from the competition?

CASE STUDY   Ryanair, more than just price

When Ryanair first began operations in 1985, the perception in the travel industry was that they were just another low-cost carrier trying to compete with the big boys in the world of aviation. However, they are and always have been much more than that. Ryanair's use of multiple channels to connect to their growing customer base has played a major part in building their business to the success it is today.

Ryanair delivers a strong business proposition: it recognized from the start that building an extensive network of destinations would grow volume. Ryanair is now one of Europe's top airlines in terms of passengers carried, with more than 130 million customers a year on more than 2,000 daily flights from 86 bases, connecting 215 destinations in 37 countries.

To continue to be highly competitive, Ryanair has also made efforts to invest in the best aircraft available. The existing fleet consists of more than 400 Boeing 737-800 aircraft, with more on order. The net result of this strategy will enable Ryanair to lower fares further, and to grow traffic to 160 million customers annually by 2024 (https://www.ryanair.com/ie/en/useful-info/about-ryanair/fleet). The fatality-free airline also leads the field as the world's safest airline, with its 33-year safety record (https://www.independent.co.uk/travel/news-and-advice/southwest-airlines-engine-explosion-passenger-death-emergency-landing-ryanair-worlds-safest-a8309831.html). Ryanair has made brand statements on making a difference to help the environment, pledging to reduce their carbon footprint and announcing a plan that will eliminate all non-recyclable plastics from its operations over the next five years.

For customers on board, this will mean initiatives such as a switch to wooden cutlery, bio-degradable coffee cups, and the removal of plastics from the range of in-flight products. It will also introduce a scheme to allow customers to offset the carbon cost of their flight through a voluntary donation online.

Ryanair has always focused on customer connectivity and, with an eye to continual improvements, launched its 'Always Getting Better' programme in 2014. The programme includes a wide range of customer service and digital enhancements, such as a new website and app, new uniforms, refreshed cabin interiors, allocated seating options and tailored products. In addition, to encourage customers to explore the extensive range of destinations, Ryanair also features a 'Try Somewhere New' travel hub on its website, which hosts exclusive travel guides and destination videos. By connecting with their customer base and giving people choices in this way, they are differentiating from their competitors and at the same time building loyalty.

While Ryanair continue to innovate, the one thing that won't change will be its low fares – which they promise will not be beaten – and European customers will still enjoy the biggest and best choice of destinations. This relentless focus on customers, creating an easy-to-do customer culture and using all available channels to do so, has been the secret of their success.

References and useful resources

References and further reading

Burlingham, B and Gendron, G (1989) The Entrepreneur of the Decade, *Inc.* [online] Available at: https://www.inc.com/magazine/19890401/5602.html

Calder, S (2018) Ryanair is the world's safest airline after Southwest's mid-air tragedy [online] *Independent*. Available at: https://www.independent.co.uk/travel/news-and-advice/southwest-airlines-engine-explosion-passenger-death-emergency-landing-ryanair-worlds-safest-a8309831.html

Websites

https://www.benjerry.co.uk/values
http://www.ritzcarlton.com/en/about/gold-standards

https://www.tesla.com/en_GB/about
https://www.ryanair.com/ie/en/useful-info/about-ryanair/fleet

Useful resource

https://corporate.ryanair.com/about-us/fact-and-figures/

Building your retail marketing mix

05

Key points

Use all elements of the retail marketing mix

Create a response based on the results of your market research

Make sure your people (ambassadors) are all engaged on brand message

Promote to your customers

Create a marketing calendar

Recruit the right people

Create simple business processes

Perfect your instore experience

What is the retail marketing mix?

The retail marketing mix is best described as the combination of activities that retailers use to meet the wants and needs of their customers. The overall success relies on the integration of each element and how they complement one another to communicate a consistent message to potential customers.

There are seven key questions that should be addressed to cover each aspect of the retail marketplace, set out in Figure 5.1. Remember each individual element cannot work in isolation – all elements

Figure 5.1   The retail marketing mix

should work together to ensure each potential customer converts into a sale and becomes a loyal frequent shopper.

What's your pricing policy?

This is, of course, what you charge for your product or service. However, before setting your policy, ask yourself the following questions:

- What's your target return on investment?
- Are you setting your prices to be aggressive to gain market share?
- Do you want your prices to be below your competition?

In addition, when considering pricing for your product or service, one of your primary concerns is your position in the marketplace, and what price position you want to adopt. This needs to match the customers you are targeting. Consider the following: sales of high-priced luxury items generally deliver lower volume unit sales and target a very small unique sector of the market, sometimes known as 'the one per cent'. Retailers who sell lower price goods or services will appeal to a greater audience or mass market and will therefore generate higher volume unit sales. As part of your plan, also keep in mind that higher price positioning means higher customer expectations of quality and service.

This difference can have a major business impact across many areas of your business – on your choice of location, how you communicate and the physical space requirement for your product or service.

You must monitor your competitors' pricing and examine what extra services they offer customers that may also attract them. Examples of this are found typically in the sale of mass-market products, such as multipacks, buy-one-get-one-free or larger size/better value items.

Another factor to consider is elasticity of demand or price sensitivity, which affects the buying behaviour of customers. If demand for a product changes significantly when there is a small price change then consumers of that product are considered price sensitive. If there is an incidental change in demand when there is a larger change in price, then consumers are considered less price sensitive. Interestingly, research and experience has shown us that existing customers are less sensitive about price changes than new customers.

However, this does not mean that it is a wise strategy to charge high prices. Product alternatives, customer disposable income and loyalty are all factors that require careful consideration. At some point, there is a price at which demand for any product or service will drop to zero.

What product or services are you offering?

In retail terms, your product is an item or service offered for sale that might satisfy a want or need. When seeking the product you wish to sell, you need to think about it from many different perspectives.

To ensure that the quality, design and purpose of your product match the profile of your target customer and your plans for your retail business, ask yourself the following questions:

- How is the product used?
- What are its features and the benefits to the customer?
- Have you considered the sizing and packaging of the product and its implications on space?
- Are you able to negotiate added-value guarantees and customer service offerings from your suppliers?
- Do you fully understand how the product has been made?
- What is the history of the product or service you are offering?
- What are the styles, colours or models available?
- Are there any upgrades that might be available soon?
- What is the shelf life of the product?

CASE STUDY   The Forgotten Toy Shop

The Forgotten Toy Shop is a great example of how quality, design and purpose of the products sold match the profile of the target customer.

Karen, the owner and creator of The Forgotten Toy Shop, has worked in many different sectors, but the thread that has run throughout her varied career is a passion for outstanding customer service. In launching The Forgotten Toy Shop, she wanted her customers to have an experience akin to the joy of child's play – and she strives to bring the magic of childhood into everything she does.

In 2009, Karen had just returned from travelling around Australia. With the help of some friends, she started running a market stall selling gifts and traditional toys. Eventually, she sold the last of the gifts and chose to continue to build up the range of toys. In the course of this, Karen learned that there was a large range of children's toys that are beautifully made and made to last. She became an ambassador for children's toys that could inspire creativity, discovery and imagination – and she wanted parents and grandparents to be able to reconnect with the magic of their own childhoods through sharing play with younger generations. The Forgotten Toy Shop was born. Having a detailed understanding of her customer base and a passion about toys, Karen set out to provide safe, quality products that inspire adults and children to relax into a space where kids can be kids, where people can interact, and where you can revel in the pleasure of simply spending time together.

Looking at the business now, it's clear that Karen took her passion for providing high-quality products, channelled this into a cohesive business design, and, importantly, united this with her purpose: tapping into the customer's desire to use toys and play to strengthen social and family bonds.

You'll find The Forgotten Toy Shop online at theforgottentoyshop.co.uk, where you can buy directly from the website. You'll also find its products at selected stockists and at seasonal fairs throughout the UK.

Are you selling through multiple locations?

It may sound obvious, but the place where your product or service is sold is a key part of the retail marketplace process. Many successful businesses use a combination of locations to sell to their customers; the important thing is to select locations that are easily accessible to your target customers. When determining where and how many locations in which to market your product, ask yourself the following questions:

Checklist

- ✓ Are your customers able to access an online store, either your own website or through a third party (ie eBay, Amazon)?
- ✓ Is your full product range available to buy online or do you select specific product ranges?
- ✓ Is your retail store appropriate and convenient for your target customers?
- ✓ Do you operate on a concession basis within major outlets to improve awareness/exposure?
- ✓ Do you operate a direct selling process?
- ✓ Do you try to communicate and sell to customers using telemarketing?
- ✓ Do you attend relevant trade shows? Do you sell your product and generate leads when you do attend them?
- ✓ Do you use a distributor to sell your product on your behalf? Would it be economically viable to do so?

> **Tip**
>
> Success in the retail marketplace is achieved by using a combination of retailing activities that meet the wants and needs of customers.

How do you plan to promote to your customers?

Promotional activity is a way to communicate and present your offer to potential customers to convert them into actual sales transactions at the tills. It's achieved using promotion materials or avenues where you can connect with your customer. Be a smart retailer: to successfully promote offers to your customers and potential customers, start telling them more about the benefits of your product rather than just listing the product's features.

Airports are a great example of how to promote your products or services. Travel retail is one of the most competitive marketplaces in the world. However, many people believe that having a captive market makes it easy for airport retailers to sell their goods and services. In our experience, this is generally not the case. It is true that travel retailers generate high sales and achieve some of the highest sales per square metre of space in the world. However, they must work very hard and use all their creativity for this success.

Penetration and conversion ratios are in single figures. The time pressure at airports for travellers to shop and retailers to convert is always a moveable feast – security checks, delays, and early calls to gates are a constant threat to available dwell time.

Today, travel retailers are fighting back and use several techniques other non-airport retailers could learn. Shops are positioned and designed for walk-through experiences the moment you enter departure lounges. This exposes every potential customer to the main duty- and tax-free product ranges and the greatest opportunity to convert to a sale early in the airport journey. Working with suppliers, retailers create this dynamic instore experience to great effect. Prime positions are branded and supported by digital experiences that are now commonplace for the world's top brands. Highly trained people are also key to this promotional activity and have increased sales conversion ratios. Product suppliers will also play their part and will provide free promotional product to retailers to target this very influential audience. Customer interaction as a promotional tool is the key critical success factor. Non-airport retailers can use these techniques and adapt their stores to use similar promotional methods to help drive sales.

Promotional activity is only one of the key parts of your marketing mix, but it will give you a chance to hook potentially interested customers, get them engaged with your product, and hopefully result in a successful sale. Always remember that customers only have a short time in which to absorb the message you are trying to convey to them – so keep the message short, clear and simple.

Don't rely solely on suppliers subsidising the cost of your promotional campaigns with an offer of free product or workforce. Ensure you have enough promotional budget built into your plan. By using a combination of both resources, you will extend your impact in the marketplace and will improve your sales.

The initial outlay, if your promotional idea is successful, will be well worth the increased revenue it brings in. But, as well as planning for the costs of the promotion, you must also plan for the effects of the promotion: ensure that your supply channels are able to cope with the forecasted sales demand generated from the promotion you have put in place.

Once your customer is excited about your product and your promotion, they would be extremely disgruntled and disappointed to find that they can't get hold of what you're selling because your stock has run out!

Creating a marketing calendar

A marketing calendar is a supportive tool that assists you in launching your marketing activities in a structured and thought-out manner. It can be used effectively to coordinate all your marketing activities and at the same time helps to give you an overall picture of your marketing tactics and progress for the year.

Figure 5.2   An example of a marketing calendar

Month	January				
Sales target	Units/£				
Week commencing	29	4	11	18	25
Key dates and events	New Year's Eve/Day		Industry conference		Valentine's Day
Sales					
Sales pomotions	Sales promo (offer)	Sales promo (offer)	Sales promo (offer)	Sales promo (offer)	Sales promo (offer)
Staff incentive scheme	Sales	Sales	Sales	Sales	Sales
Printed collateral – flyers, brochures, etc	Flyers	Flyers			Brochures
Public Relations					
Product launches, special events and sponsorships			Industry conference		
Press releases – national/local	Local PR				
Online					
Search engine optimization – keyword/search	Keyword/search advertising				
Online auctions/ stores	Online auction and stores				
Directory listings and classified	Online directory listings and classified				
Affiliate websites	Affiliate websites				

(continued)

Figure 5.2 (Continued)

Month	January				
Sales target	Units/£				
Week commencing	29	4	11	18	25
Social media – Twitter, Facebook, etc	Facebook Announce	Pre-conference tweets	Updates	Post-conference tweets	Photos
Blog/RSS	Visit us during sale period and receive extra 10% off		Daily conference recap	Upcoming sales promo	
Email	Visit us during sale period and receive extra 10% off			Upcoming sales promo	
Website messaging	Visit us during sale period and receive extra 10% off			Upcoming sales promo	Online coupon
Podcast				Sales highlights	
Mobile			Campaign offer code – product info		
Advertising					
TV			Campaign		
Local radio			Local campaign		
Print			Product info		
Outdoor	Teaser for sale				
Research					
Customer surveys		Profiling		Satisfaction survey	Feedback
Competition		Review		Review	
Store layout	Review		Review		
Product placement	Monitor	Monitor	Monitor	Monitor	Monitor
Marketing effectiveness	Measure				Review

For a more detailed example of a marketing calendar and a year-long marketing calendar template, go to www.koganpage.com/retail-startup.

A marketing calendar can be used to focus your efforts, making sure that you are using every opportunity to give your business the best possible chance of success. A marketing calendar should be tailored to your individual retailer needs – international, national or local, depending on your business needs – and can be broken down into weeks of the year to address the marketing activities that will take place in each week.

As some products lend themselves to seasonal demand, there is an opportunity to create added interest in your store by planning tactical promotional activity relevant to your customers. Speak to your supply chain distributors about timing and up-and-coming product launches. Based on this information, you can develop a seasonal calendar to promote to your customers.

When planning, consider both the market and the environment, as well as all the promotional channels that are available to you. Once you've done this, you can decide on the type and timing of your activity. As part of this process you may choose to promote your product or service through channels such as advertising on local radio and in newspapers, personal selling, sampling instore, direct marketing and social media. As a lower cost option, make and use connections both with your existing customers and other businesses near or connected to yours. You can tap into the value of your existing customers by using endorsements from them to promote your product. This can be a very effective route. Your links with other businesses can be useful if you enter into cross-promotional ventures. This can increase your reach many times over and creates real value for your customers. A recent example of this is Butlers Chocolates and its partnership with Emirates airline. Working together meant first-class passengers received a first-class product, Emirates reduced costs and Butlers got brand exposure to a very exclusive worldwide audience travelling between 160 destinations (https://www.rte.ie/news/business/2018/1023/1006141-butlers-chocolate-emirates-deal/).

Once you begin implementing the activities planned in your marketing calendar, you can also use the calendar to measure and review the effectiveness of your marketing activities on a regular basis and adjust where required. If your marketing calendar highlights an activity that is working well, then increase the frequency of that activity. Likewise, if things aren't going to plan, reduce activity and seek alternatives. Make sure you are continually monitoring the results, and don't forget to talk to your customers about what they liked or disliked. Involve your staff – they can also help you to build on your successes and learn from any promotions that did not do quite so well.

Whatever channels you choose through which to promote your product or service, the most important point to highlight for any new start-up is to keep your message clear and consistent. Customers like things simple and easy to understand, and, in our experience, promotions that follow this route are often the most successful ones.

Are you recruiting the right people?

The people you employ can make or break your retail business. Before you even begin the hiring process, you must make sure you fully understand the impact your people have on your existing and potential new customers and the impact it has on your business performance. Steve Jobs said of his recruitment strategy: 'I noticed that the dynamic range between what an average person could accomplish and what the best person could accomplish was 50 or 100 to 1. Given that, you're well advised to go after the cream of the cream... A small team of A+ players can run circles round a giant team of B and C players' (https://www.adventureassoc.com/steve-jobs-recruiting/).

When recruiting, ask yourself:

- How do you plan to find the right people?
- Do you know how many people are required?
- What is the service culture in your retail business?
- How are you planning to see this communicated and adopted by the people you employ?
- Do you recognize developing relationships with your people is a two-way process?
- How do you intend to communicate your brand message to your staff?

- How do you want the brand message carried through in the way staff interact with customers?

- Have you created clear channels enabling your staff to give you valuable feedback about the product and your customers? This is how two-way communication can have a considerable, positive impact on the motivation levels of your people.

- Do you plan to both invest in staff abilities and training, and share the financial success of your business? Highly involved people, fully trained and who understand the products and services you offer will deliver higher levels of sales, service and engagement.

Once on board, your staff engagement strategy should be a major part of the business and should help drive sales, the profits of which you will be able to share with your people. Again, a positive-feedback loop is in place. One way to retain people is by keeping them motivated, and by maintaining their interest in their job *and* the business by empowering them. Within limits – as ultimately it is you who is driving the brand and doing the forward planning – you should allow all your people to make business decisions that benefit customers. When frontline people can give this kind of input, they will value even more highly the information you communicate with them about how the business is performing. If your people have had a hand in the direction the business is taking, they will take an interest in how effective different ideas have been, which of course becomes apparent when you look at the bottom-line sales.

Communicating business performance regularly will help to motivate and engage individuals to work as part of a team. Keep this process simple – agree some key performance indicators (KPIs) that are relevant for your business. For example, set sales targets for the week or month, then record the number of customers entering the store versus the number of customers buying. The penetration versus conversion ratio KPI will give you great insight into the shopping behaviour of your customers, and by monitoring this particular KPI you can ask the questions: Why do we have many customers entering the store but not buying? Do we have the right product or services available? Creating this involvement culture will pay dividends in the future by transforming your team into active participants who will want to be part of the business success.

Are you making your business processes simple?

In marketing terms, 'process' refers to how easy you are to do business with. Put simply, it's how well your business systems are designed for you and the customer. Peter Drucker famously said 'Efficiency is doing things right, effectiveness is doing the right things' (https://www.toolshero.com/toolsheroes/peter-drucker/).

This starts at the most fundamental level, such as your opening hours, and extends right through the business. Having robust, well-thought-through processes is essential to any growing business. To analyse your current processes or to set your processes in place, consider the following questions:

Checklist

- ✓ Do your hours of operation match your customer requirements?
- ✓ Do you have systems in place to respond to customer enquiries promptly?
- ✓ Are your processes simple, effective and fully understood by your people?
- ✓ Do you have a stock management and delivery process in place that meets the forecast demands of your products and services?
- ✓ Do you have contingency process plans in place that cover all events?
- ✓ Do you measure the performance of your retail space to increase productivity?
- ✓ What system or process do you adopt to manage your customer database?
- ✓ What logistics process do you have in place to manage the sales distribution of your products and services?

Is your instore experience the best it can be?

The physical environment of your store creates the first and lasting impression on your customers. It is essential to ensure your retail outlet or sales channel reflects the quality of the products and service that you offer. Think carefully about the initial impression as well as the final impression your customers get upon entering and exiting your retail environment. Compare this with your competitors. As well as ideas about your brand and how you wish it to be perceived, you should be able to use transaction sales data to measure the performance of your existing physical environment. Sending out a clear message about your store and products relies on making sure that you are consistent across all elements of your instore retail environment across all customer touch points.

Think beyond only providing the basics in your store. How can you use sensory techniques (smell, taste, sound, touch) to enhance your store environment? Caterers have long used the smell of baking bread or coffee to entice new customers into their units with great success. Background music or store lighting can also greatly enhance the customer experience.

Welcoming the customer as they enter is again an important first impression, but be aware of the over-eager staff member approach, which can also create a negative first impression by making the customer feel set upon and uncomfortable. The secret to success here is to be natural and to find the right balance for your customer type. Train your staff to encourage shoppers to touch and try your product, and make sure you have sufficient stock available for this – it's a big selling point.

Consider offering additional services to match your customer requirements wherever possible. This could include, for example, customer toilets, seating, changing facilities, play areas, café, lifts, car parking or transportation. Another important factor to consider in your retail environment is your obligation to meet accessibility requirements.

According to research conducted by the Department for Work and Pensions, the top three most difficult experiences for disabled people based on accessibility are shopping, eating and drinking out. Another study by the Extra Costs Commission stated that poor customer service has led to three-quarters of disabled people (and the friends or family accompanying them) to leave a shop, taking their purses and wallets with them. The study deduced that this meant as much as £420 million a week in sales is lost to UK businesses as a result. (http://www.bmmagazine.co.uk/news/three-four-disabled-consumers-say-left-shop-due-bad-customer-service/)

By law, you must make sure your store is fully accessible and compliant for all customers, but smart retailers don't just comply with these requirements – they exceed them. Remember also that not all disabilities are instantly recognizable; make your staff aware of this and encourage them not to make assumptions. While getting it wrong can be costly in terms of sales, it will impact hugely in reputation. Reputational cost is even greater as many people will spread the word via social media and other channels. This instant damage to your brand and business could be incalculable.

As a starting point, find out the facts in your local community about disability associations, and use these resources to learn more about needs and requirements. Then, make your staff aware of these important findings. Even better, get your staff to attend and learn first-hand. Always include these considerations in your plans and expect a major lost opportunity if you don't.

References and useful resources

References and further reading

Business Matters (2017) 'Three in four disabled consumers say they have left a shop due to bad customer service' [online]. Available at: https://www.bmmagazine.co.uk/news/three-four-disabled-consumers-say-left-shop-due-bad-customer-service

Ramsay, D (2015) 'Steve Jobs on Recruiting', Adventure Associates [online]. Available at: https://www.adventureassoc.com/steve-jobs-recruiting

RTE.ie (2018) 'Butlers Chocolates latest brand to win Emirates deal' [online]. Available at: https://www.rte.ie/news/business/2018/1023/1006141-butlers-chocolate-emirates-deal

Van Vliet, V (2010) 'Peter Drucker', ToolsHero [online]. Available at: https://www.toolshero.com/toolsheroes/peter-drucker

Website

https://www.theforgottentoyshop.co.uk

Winning in retail – know your market, know your customer

06

Key points

Ask key questions about your market

Ask key questions about your customer

Monitor changes and keep your knowledge up to date

Capturing marketplace insights

Smart retail businesses should have a detailed knowledge of the market in which they operate and the customers that they buy for and sell to. To market your business effectively, you need to establish where your product or service is positioned in the marketplace, how your business operates in the current financial climate and how competitors are likely to affect your overall performance.

Your ability to succeed relies on your knowledge and understanding of your current and potential customers, the products and services that they demand and the competition that exists from other businesses. Ensure you incorporate this into your research brief as this will enable you to effectively plan for customer targeting, effective selling, supplier competition and new business opportunities.

Capturing market insights will help you to build a much more in-depth knowledge of the marketplace in which you operate. It will help to change your understanding from what 'you think' is happening (perception) into a validated set of facts.

Start by asking yourself the questions from the 'Know your market' checklist. This will help you to compile the relevant information to enable you to make the right decisions for your retail business.

Know your market checklist

- ✓ What is the size, scale and value of the market you operate in?
- ✓ What segment are you in and what is your market share?
- ✓ What is the size, scale and value of the competition within the market you operate in?
- ✓ Do you operate in multiple markets?
- ✓ Are you affected by seasonality?
- ✓ What is the current overall market demand for your product or service?
- ✓ What are the current economic and market trends within your market?
- ✓ Are you aware of any market intelligence for new, upcoming products or services from competitors?
- ✓ Do you regularly monitor the competition for price, operations and how they communicate to customers?
- ✓ Are you aware of the current and any forthcoming changes in legislation that could affect your market?

You should also consider how you are gathering and recording information, as well as your process and the frequency at which you review all the data you have gathered. Maintaining and expanding your knowledge of the market in which you operate should be undertaken on an ongoing basis and is essential to your overall marketing plan.

Connecting with customers

To influence new or existing customers, you first need to gain a thorough understanding of their decision-making process. In today's always-on marketing and retail climate, most retailers are faced with an incredibly broad and diverse customer base. At times, the thought and effort of trying to capture and understand this information can be overwhelming, but it should be prioritized. Failing to ask – and answer – key questions about your customers can lead to many missed retail sales opportunities.

Know your customer checklist

✓ Do you really know and understand who your customers are?

✓ Do you know what they buy and the reason for buying it?

✓ How do your customers use the product/service they buy?

✓ Do your customers expect a tailored product or service to match their needs?

✓ Are you aware of your customer's ability to access greater product information through technology and what effect that has on your business?

✓ How do you communicate with your customers?

✓ Are you aware of the different retail customer profiles and the different reasons each one buys a product or service?

✓ What are you doing to satisfy customers who demand retail products and services that not only deliver a basic need, but also provide additional positive benefits?

✓ How do you establish the differences between one set of customers and another and ensure you match your retail product or service to your existing or target group of new customers?

✓ Have you segmented your customers by who they are and what they want to make the process of exploiting retail opportunities easier?

✓ Are you monitoring changes in your customers' needs and shopping patterns to ensure that you can deliver for today and predict what they want in the future?

To simplify the process of customer research, and to combat the scale of diversity within your customer base, it can help to approach this in steps.

Step 1

Break down and analyse your customers in different groups or segments. For example, using:

- geographic grouping, which may be by country, region or proximity to your store:
- demographic grouping, by disposable income, age, gender;
- behavioural grouping, which aims to understand actual usage, spending habits and loyalty of specific customers. You might find geographic and demographic data correlate to this data.

Step 2

Begin asking yourself the questions from our 'Know your customer' checklist for each customer group. Answer as many as you can – and pay attention to where you have the largest knowledge gaps. These may become focus areas in your marketing plan.

Step 3

By building this knowledge layer by layer, you will begin to understand your customer groups as distinct from one another. This will give you the confidence to target them individually with products and services that are relevant to them – so start brainstorming the most appropriate products and marketing strategies for each group. Not only will this improve your confidence when speaking of your various customer groups, but, most importantly, this will be more profitable for you in the long run.

Step 4

Throughout this process, ensure you are keeping detailed and ongoing records of this valuable customer insight information. It will become an invaluable resource to which you can refer in the future.

CASE STUDY PizzaExpress

PizzaExpress started over 50 years ago when founder Peter Boizot identified a gap in the market coupled with a strategy to build a deep understanding of customers' needs and then create innovative ways to satisfying them. This is why its strategy has stood the test of time. Boizot, through his vision, perseverance and making it easy for his customers, has created a long-term major brand success.

His leadership skills have been consistently demonstrated in his strong determination, and in the way he never let bureaucracy get in the way. This ethos was the guiding light for all the PizzaExpress family and still is today. Boizot would stand firm on his plans, but at the same time he was never afraid to adopt change, especially when he knew it was what his customers were demanding. He recognized very early on that his success was contingent upon keeping the process simple and combining other experiences for his customers.

He also recognized the strength of community spirit and building pride in the local area. He knew his local customer base would develop into loyal customers and would play a vital part in its success. He started a trend designing each restaurant in its own style to be relevant and specific to the local area.

Delivering amazing food and creating customer experiences are areas that PizzaExpress is passionate about. However, it has also recognized the importance of delivering this on a consistent basis. This cannot be achieved by what is said in words alone, but requires a high-performing team of people who interact with customers daily. Its recruitment strategy of creating equal opportunities has attracted and built a strong and diverse team who can relate to and communicate with customer groups from all different backgrounds, ages, genders, ethnicity or national origins. It is truly a diverse customer profile served by a diverse Pizza Express family, and it's all part of its vision to have a world made happier by pizza.

To help build a detailed understanding of the behaviour of its target audience and demographic across the entire social spectrum, a social research strategy was created for PizzaExpress. It outlined where the noise was being created around its brand and how much was being generated across each channel. This data capture was invaluable and helped create the best way for the company to interact and engage with its followers.

The PizzaExpress customer engagement strategy is extensive and is, in our opinion, a two-way communication, delivering a win-win result. Not only does it give the customer the opportunity to feed back, it allows PizzaExpress to work to improve the quality of its product and service.

Customers can either connect with the customer services team online or by phone or talk directly to the restaurant they visited. Customers can also choose the 'Take the survey' option, which allows for a more detailed exchange. Online, there is an option to 'Ask anything', which prompts customers by highlighting the top five questions. There is even an option for 'Want to talk to us about something else?', which cover topics such as marketing and suppliers' questions.

Capturing this data and building up this knowledge over time has resulted in PizzaExpress gaining a deep understanding of its customers. This invaluable information has allowed the business to respond quicker to customers and to take appropriate action against any competitor or threats in the marketplace in which they operate.

References and useful resources

Website

https://www.pizzaexpress.com

Understanding the basic principles of shopping

07

Key points

Research your customer behaviour and shopping patterns

Create a store layout and monitor sales performance

Optimize your people for customer satisfaction

What makes potential customers buy?

The aim for those working in the retail industry is to learn what makes people buy products or services. Successful retailers are well-versed in the modern-day techniques of persuading customers to buy. Understanding some of the basic principles of shopping and the reasons customers make purchases can make a huge impact on the success you have as a retail business.

Research shopping behaviour

Finding out more about your customer instore behaviour and shopping patterns is the key to success. Developing a detailed understanding of why customers do or do not buy instore, whether they default to online, or whether they are willing to purchase either instore or online can help you to take positive actions. Consider the following questions:

- Are your customers buying for price, convenience or range?
- Do they have a special need or event to buy for?

By building connections with customers, you can create loyalty and build your sales over time. There are many reasons customers do or don't buy, but the four key retailer influencers on why customers will shop with you are listed below:

- Do you have the range and quality of products they're looking for?
- Are you competitive on price?
- Does the instore experience match the customer's expectations?
- Is high-quality customer service delivered by your people on a consistent basis?

Customers' influencers are also driven by social reasons such as lifestyle, time and disposable income. Some quantitative information on instore behaviour and shopping patterns can be obtained through the introduction of camera or count technology, or via instore observation techniques. Combining this data with qualitative research, which could involve face-to-face feedback gathered instore, so that you gain a real understanding of what customers think about your store will help you to make changes to deliver productive results.

Many years ago, one of the authors of this book was involved in a major airport research project that monitored potential customers' heart rate at each point in the journey process from leaving home to boarding the plane. The objective was to identify the best place along this journey to engage with the customer, and therefore influence their shopping pattern. It was already an accepted fact that when customers had more time and were in a relaxed frame of mind, their spend transactions would increase. However, for many years resources were deployed in all the wrong areas and the return on investment was heading rapidly southwards.

The results of this airport research project were fascinating. Heart rates were higher than normal when people were still at home, due to the anxiety of travel and arriving at their end destination, as well as making sure everything was attended to at home while they were away. After arriving at the airport, this pattern of accelerated heart rates continued, but dropped slightly during the check-in process and as bags were handed over. This was followed by a significant surge in heart rate through security control. It was only when customers entered departure lounges, after all the processing checkpoints of airport travel were over, that their heart rates dropped back to their resting level. If you could draw the results on a graph, the heart rate of the customer would look like a roller coaster with peaks and dips. Where the line on the graph becomes more consistent is where customers are more receptive to marketing messaging. Logically, the conclusion was that this was the zone to promote products and services to potential customers.

This new research delivered quantitative data, and insight based on facts, which enabled retailers to alter the deployment of their scarce resources, money and people, and begin to reverse the trend on the return on investment. A lesson had been learned and resources reallocated to great effect.

With this research in mind, think now about your own store. Consider:

- Are my customers relaxed and calm instore? If not, why not?
- How does my customer shop in my store?
- How much time do they spend instore?
- What are my peak periods, by day, week and month?
- Why does a customer make a purchase?
- Why don't they make a purchase?
- How many customers enter my store and leave without making a purchase?
- How many customers interact with staff?
- What's my instore queue length?
- Is the store easy to navigate, and the customer journey smooth?
- Where is customer behaviour telling me to place promotional items? At aisle ends, or at till points, or both?
- If needed, where should the changing facilities be positioned?

By understanding and gathering results for this kind of research and evaluating your answers, you will learn that customers have different buying behaviours by time of day, week and year. The information you gather will help you to increase knowledge of your customers and thus enable you to adopt new tactics and working practices that will both increase the conversion of potential customers into sales and increase the transaction value per shopper.

Organize your instore space

You can use your new-found knowledge of shoppers to plan your store layout and ensure your customers navigate their way through it on your terms. The aim, above all, is not to confuse your customer: keep it simple.

First, map each physical touch point in the customer journey and implement ideas to improve the experience at each stage. This should start street side, and you should challenge yourself to think about how your shop front or shop window first appears to the prospective customer. Consider:

- What makes my potential customer choose my store rather than the competition?
- What does the look and feel of the windows or the open door tell you about your store?

Next, think about what happens when the customer enters the store. Clearly positioned wayfinding signage will help customers to navigate your store. Once you have a system in place, monitor it by tracking your customers' behaviour instore and use your findings to work out if the layout of your store is maximizing your sales.

Your primary concern should be that the space in your store creates a comfortable experience for your customers – this means that different sections and different products should be positioned on fixtures that maximize your sales. Conversely, products that are not selling will be highlighted and your store will become more productive overall.

You should have dedicated, tactical promotional areas that are alternated on a regular basis – and ensure your product labelling gives your customers all the relevant information they want and need to make the purchase. You should also consider using lighting to attract customers to specific products or adopting sensory tools to allow customers to experience merchandise before they buy.

It's also important to measure the dwell time of customers in your store and to find out what is driving this in either a positive or negative direction. If over a period you see dwell time declining, try providing your customers with other facilities like free Wi-Fi, a café, or toilets, and try to build the dwell time for their visit. This will create opportunities for your frontline sales people to have more time to engage with prospective customers and convert them into purchasers.

Most importantly, make sure to continually check in on your processes and analyse your instore performance, considering the points made in this chapter. You can use the following as a checklist of points for which you should endeavour always to have an answer, or improvements in mind.

Checklist

- ✓ Think about how you currently communicate with your customers, and if you're effectively tracking their responses.
- ✓ Consider the methods you use to build customer loyalty, and how you can extend your welcome beyond the footprint of your store.
- ✓ Always remember the importance of the first and last impressions of your store. Upon entry, give your customers enough time to adjust to your retail environment.
- ✓ At the point of making a sale, ensure you accept all methods of payment to satisfy your customers' individual requirements.
- ✓ Optimize your staff for customer satisfaction; the people you have front of house can make a huge difference to your customers' experience.
- ✓ Make sure you deploy your full resources to match the time patterns that your customer has available to shop, and in a time frame that suits their requirements.

✓ Ensure you have provided enough resources for your customers to complete their purchases. This means having the right balance of staff available at peak times of the day and different days of the week, ensuring maximin efficiency of staff and customer engagement. There is no point having a great looking store full of potential customers and not enough people on hand to convert them into sales. Everyone must be ready to welcome potential customers to maximize business in these critical periods.

✓ Encourage your staff to engage with your customers and make sure that you are aware of any cultural and language differences.

✓ Train your staff (they're also your ambassadors) to make sure they can communicate and overcome any barriers in order that all customers have an informative, enjoyable experience in store.

Tip

Your primary concern should be that your store space creates an enjoyable, comfortable experience for your customers. Look after your customers or someone else will.

Attracting and retaining customers online, using on-brand content and social media

08

Key points

Create an on-brand website

Engage with social media – but don't overdo it

Get your content shared

Useful tools available to you

Mistakes to avoid; the don't list

Creating an on-brand website

In this chapter, we'll look at the best ways to navigate your way through the digital maze. The key to attracting and retaining more customers is through effective communication and supply using all available channels; this obviously includes online. As discussed in previous chapters, understanding the basic principles of the retail marketing mix, knowing your customer and market intimately as well as understanding the drivers behind customer behaviour and buying patterns is the first step. Next, you need to know what your customers want and make it available online.

Creating a website for your retail business is a key part of communicating with and selling to your customers. Nowadays, customers assume you have a website – or at least a social media page fulfilling the same functions – and they will use it to find out more about your business at a time and a place convenient to them. Customers use websites to compare your offer to your competitors' in a very short amount of time and using very little effort. Make sure you follow the basic principles for your website to use it effectively to attract and retain more customers. Whether building your website yourself or enlisting a designer or developer to help you, use the following checklist as a guide.

Checklist

✓ Keep it simple and easy to navigate.

✓ Ensure the look and feel of the design reflect the products and services you are offering.

✓ Make sure each page of your site has something valuable to offer.

✓ Include a 'Call to action' on each page to prompt customer activity.

✓ Make sure the content is always up-to-date and relevant.

✓ Include contact information.

✓ Monitor visitors to your website using online tools such as Google Analytics so you can learn more about your customers and which parts of the site they are accessing.

✓ Pay attention to search engine optimization (SEO) to boost your online presence.

✓ If you are operating an online store, make sure this is regularly monitored and everything is working as it should.

✓ Invest in a secure online ordering system.

Apps

Apps are a hot topic in marketing circles and as a start-up retailer you could also consider creating your own. Mobile retail is already pivotal to the industry – whether customers are navigating to your website, using an app or engaging with your social media. The advantage of an app is that it's not just about shopping – it's about additional content, and users can save it and return to it. It can also be more effective than a website or social media pages in developing a loyalty programme. An example of an app we really like is from designer handbag and accessory designer, Radley London. We'd recommend taking a look at it to gain an understanding of how an effective app looks and works (and pay attention to how they have selected complementary products).

Using social media effectively

Retailing online can reach a worldwide audience, so constantly considering how customers are going to search and find your products and store online can grow your business hugely. If you use social media strategically, it can bring customers to your website from unexpected places.

A social media strategy should be a part of your annual marketing planning: a well-run Twitter account, Instagram account or Facebook page that talks to and hears from customers regularly, without overloading them, is a form of almost-free advertising. Sharing between groups and individuals can take your message to new customers with very little effort on your part. Social media also allows you to collect valuable feedback from customers. You can use online conversations and interactions with customers or potential customers to gauge whether they understand your brand, what is attracting them to your brand, and how you can make the vital connection between them visiting your website and purchasing from it or visiting your physical store.

You don't need to be on every channel, and it's important not to overstretch yourself. The strain of updating and responding on too many channels will wear you down and the quality of your material will suffer; people can spot when it starts to sound forced or repetitive. Choose the networks that best define your brand and resonate with your audience and concentrate on working well on them – it's far better to master those than be a master of none.

There are millions of brands using social media and the challenge is to keep your customers coming back for more. To do this, you need to care about your customers' wants and needs, listen to them, and encourage interaction on your channels. Keep an eye on your competitors and use this knowledge to improve your own channels – always give people a reason to follow you.

Twitter, LinkedIn, Facebook and Pinterest all have different audiences with different expectations so choose your platforms with care and then become expert on those.

CASE STUDY   Fashercise: where fashion meets exercise

A marvellous example of an influential new business operating effectively as a multi-channel retailer is Fashercise. Alongside its showroom in London, the online platform sells luxury sportswear from international independent designers. As well as functioning as a retail platform, the website also features an online magazine, with blog-style articles covering food, music, technology and wellness, as well as fashion. The website conveys a strong brand message – promoting 'real girls living real lives'.

Founder Alexandra Vanthournout was challenged to run a half-marathon. She accepted and spent months training for it. With her background in fashion, Alexandra asked herself how she could combine fashion and exercise. The brand Fashercise was born. Its business ethos is firmly rooted in the belief that fashion and exercise can work together seamlessly and that, above all, exercise should be fun and make its customers feel great. Alex describes social media as the brand's primary means of communicating with customers and therefore has a comprehensive social media strategy across Instagram, Facebook, Pinterest and Twitter.

Instagram is the most important platform for the brand as it hosts short videos that showcase the fit of the clothes. The Fashercise Instagram feed is also transactional, taking advantage of Instagram's shoppable posts function, and allowing Alex to track clicks and sales.

Getting your content shared

Once you've started setting out a social media strategy and planning content for your online platforms, the next thing to think about is getting your content shared. This will help to build a greater audience for your business. Positive engagement means your social media channels are circulating authentic customer reviews, which will build your reputation over time. When producing social media content, keep in mind the following points:

- quality over quantity;
- be original;
- be concise;
- use pictures and videos;
- post content at key times.

Prioritizing quality over quantity and an unwavering focus and commitment to creating and publishing content should always take precedence over bolstering your number of social media followers. A small yet loyal group of followers that is engaged and enjoys your content is more likely to share it compared to a huge group that scrolls straight past it. Creating great content and being original go hand-in-hand. If you're telling people what they already know or posting things they've seen before, they are not going to share your content. If it was great the first time they saw it, they've probably already shared it. Creating original content doesn't necessarily mean that all of your ideas have to be brand new; try looking at things differently or presenting them in a fresh way.

While different social media platforms offer different functionalities and word limits, it's important to always be concise, no matter what length you are writing to. If this is something you struggle with, a Twitter limit can actually be a benefit to you. Short posts capture attention quickly and are easy for followers to respond to and share. The type of content you're posting plays a part as well, so consider whether you might also include an image, video, link or poll. Visuals are more likely to capture the attention of, and be shared by, a follower over a post entirely made up of text. Try to post pictures connected with your area, product or service, and remember to stand out – humorous, thought-provoking or informative posts are what keep your followers interested. Posting content at certain times of the day are better than others. In general, it's accepted that morning and afternoon commuter times, lunchtime and evenings are best on weekdays, while afternoons perform better on weekends. This will vary depending on your product and audience, so it is recommended that you undertake your own testing to see what time most engages your audience. Once you've established your key times, be sure to regularly post during these times to maximize effectiveness.

Useful tools available

Once you begin using social media for your business, you'll quickly realize that each platform displays visual content differently – some will have restrictions, specific dimensions or orientation specifications. One app you might consider to help optimize your images is Canva. It's available for iPhone, iPad and Android and is great for quickly creating correctly sized images for use across different social media platforms. The app lets you add images straight from your camera roll and select from various templates, including sizes for Instagram, Facebook, Twitter and Pinterest, then upload straight to these respective apps. If you were otherwise resizing the same image many times over to use across your different platforms, this will be a big time-saver. You can also use Canva's available layouts to design, share and print business cards, logos and presentations, among other things, if you're undertaking these design tasks yourself.

A social media scheduler, such as Hootsuite or TweetDeck, can also be a handy time-saver. Hootsuite supports social network integrations for Twitter, Facebook, Instagram, LinkedIn, Google+ and YouTube, while TweetDeck, originally an independent app, has since been acquired by Twitter and is now integrated into Twitter's interface.

When you're feeling productive, you can hammer out lots of content and then schedule that content for publication. Scheduling tools can also alert you when your business is mentioned on a social media platform and help you to quarantine negative mentions of your business. This can make executing customer service on multiple social media accounts much more manageable.

If using stock imagery, or a mix of stock and original imagery, image libraries can be a helpful resource. Some, such as Getty Images and Shutterstock, can be used on a pay per image, prepaid or subscription basis. Others, such as Unsplash, StockSnap, and Pexels, offer image libraries that at the time of writing can be used free of charge, for both commercial and non-commercial purposes. It's worth keeping in mind, though, that an overuse of stock imagery can be very identifiable – original images will usually resonate better with an audience.

Getting started with social media channels

If you haven't used social media before, it can be helpful to have an overview of some of the main platforms. We've included a few here, but it's also worth asking others in your industry what their experience has been or, if you're willing to allocate budget, enlisting the help of a one-time or ongoing social media advisor.

Twitter

Focus on having a clear biography and username that captures exactly what it is your business does. You can also include keyword hashtags in your biography, as well as a link to your main website. Both can help boost your Twitter postings and reactions in search engine results.

When posting, Twitter's character limit per post is now 280 characters and doesn't include URLs or Twitter handles (@name). Including tags to other Twitter users as well as hashtags in your posts help with visibility.

Instagram

On Instagram, you can set up either a personal account or a business account. Both are free, but the business option gives you more useful features such as activity data analytics.

Once you're into posting, frequency is key and we'd recommend posting at least once a day, if possible. There's no need to be shy with the text, as on Twitter, as the character limit on an Instagram post is 2,200, which will give you room for around 300–400 words. You can use up to 30 hashtagged keywords on a post, and we would recommend either placing them in a comment underneath your text caption, so the reader does not get swamped with keywords, or a few lines below your caption so there is some visible separation. If you use Instagram, you'll already have seen brands using this approach.

Helpfully, Instagram tells you the number of posts out there using each keyword – so keep an eye on hashtags with very high results for numbers of posts: it means yours is likely to get lost. To help with engagement and discoverability, try to always include a location when posting.

Overall, curate your content carefully and check that each post supports your overall aims and message.

Help with hashtags

If you ever see a hashtag and are unsure on what it means, an online tool like Tagdef can help. It's essentially a dictionary for hashtags, where you can simply look up your tag and the website will return a definition. Online hashtag generators, like Hashtagify, can also help to suggest the most popular or trending hashtags on your topic or brand area, if you're getting stuck for ideas. You'll find, though, that practice and keeping an eye on competitors is the best way to gain an understanding of the hashtags that work best for your business – niche hashtags will be more effective for targeting a small, engaged audience than generic hashtags with hundreds of thousands of results.

Google Maps and Google My Business

Registering with Google My Business for free will give your business a public identity with a Business Profile on Google. This doesn't re-place your business's website, but complements it because once you've created a Google My Business listing your business information will appear in Google maps and Google search functions. (Obviously, you need to have a physical location for this to be applicable.) Once your business is listed, your Business Profile can also host reviews – so encourage your customers to leave their comments. Social proof is becoming more and more important, as discerning customers seek out the genuine and authentic people and services. Community-drive programme, Google Local Guides, can also help to boost your business's presence and encouraging Local Guides to take some good pictures of your location and products can really help increase your exposure online.

Useful tools

- https://www.canva.com
- https://hootsuite.com
- https://tweetdeck.twitter.com
- https://tagdef.com/en
- https://hashtagify.me/hashtag/tbt

Social media mistakes to avoid

- Tell the truth about your proposition, your life and your objectives.
- Always be authentic, because you are authentic. Always give the impression that it is your 'handwriting' all over the business, because it must be.
- Always describe your business the way you would in a normal conversation: Never come over as 'mechanical'.
- You are a professional now – sound and look like one. Remember, you are being judged against the very best.
- Always remain cool, even if you think you are being unfairly treated. Losing it loses your customer.

- Always focus on yourself and your business. Relentlessly talk about the great things and services you offer. It will be your customers who ultimately decide whether to follow you or a competitor.

- Never copy and paste. You will never know where content originates.

- You run a business. If your customers want contact, always, always respond.

- Social media is an everyday job. Content may not need changing every day, but it must be looked at.

- Set up a comments page and invite posts. Feedback from customers is the best feedback you can get; analyse it methodically.

- Be on the lookout for bad language. Remove it.

- Don't try and operate without a clear social media policy. Social media in business only works when it has clearly defined parameters. These should include information such as who will be responsible for what.

- Know what you're doing in the world of data protection. Check this out: https://www.gov.uk/data-protection-your-business.

- A business's social media strategy and output should never be interwoven with your private life. They don't mix.

- Your social media strategy must always reflect the 'personality' of your business. Never allow the essential operations of the business to get in the way of ever-positive communications.

CASE STUDY   Sophie Hulme

It was the launch of Instagram that changed the fortune of Sophie Hulme, a young graduate from a university close to London. Hulme believed that consumers were tiring of over-the-top logos on handbags and so she set about designing attractive, functional and simply designed bags in unusual colours. She wanted to use only good-quality leather and made sure the skins were properly dyed so as not to lose their colour.

Hulme undertook extensive research in the market and knew that she had to source leather from the best tanneries. This led her to visit Lineapelle, the Italian trade fair renowned for exhibiting the top producers of leather. Hulme pitched her prices at affordable levels – way below the prices demanded from leading designer brands. She found her niche and gradually began to build a brand and attract a following. Hulme now designs her collections in London and produces her bags in Italy and Hungary because that is where she found the manufacturing skills she wanted.

She cautiously expanded online using Instagram, approaching it like a magazine, packed with content and information. She uses social media, as well as her regularly updated website, in harmony with her brand's physical presence. She has recently opened a specialty store in a fashionable street in London, allowing her to display her collections to their full potential as well as to test new designs in small quantities.

This story precisely illustrates how Hulme identified a market opportunity and trusted her design skills to create a product that consumers would buy. She very sensibly went through the processes of deciding early on whether to trade online or in a store: she chose the former. She then researched the materials she would need and the factories able to produce her collection to the standards she demanded and within the price band she chose.

What we find so impressive is the gradual and methodical approach Hulme adopted. She walked and did not run. She developed her brand step by step, building on the successes and learning from the failures. Before she opened her shop, she trialled a pop-up in central London that went on longer than planned. That experience gave her the motivation and confidence she needed to take a permanent shop. Sophie Hulme's is a very inspiring and impressive story and most importantly provides ample examples of a methodical and business-like approach coupled with focus and personal belief. The takeaway from this example is: Listen to others, take counsel but always trust yourself. You will prevail.

CASE STUDY   Grace Gould and Soda

While working for Apple, Grace Gould had a sense that many women were often patronized in the electronic sections of department stores. Having accumulated a knowledge of both retail and tech products over her career, she identified a significant gap: that no one seemed to be talking directly to women about lifestyle tech, despite women being the biggest consumers.

Gould launched Soda, School of the Digital Age, in 2017. She put together a collection of tech products she believed were useful and time-saving as well as aesthetically suited to her market. She carried over her design outlook to the beautifully presented Soda website and curated Twitter feed, developing a brand synergy that remained consistent with her overall brand position.

Despite the fact that Gould fully embraces social media, she began by trialling her ideas in a pop-up shop in London. She was encouraged by social media followers and quickly identified that forward-thinking and world-leading department stores like Selfridges might be interested in giving her collection a space. She was right and, after a year or so of trading in her pop-up, Selfridges did indeed give her products space on its tech floor. That breakthrough provided the visibility Soda needed, and Soda is now set to have products showcased in ten stores in the United States.

This is a brilliant story of niche knowledge built up in a specific field turned to an original business idea launched by a creative and tenacious owner. Gould's systematic approach of planning, research, sourcing, market relevance, shopping behaviour, social media marketing, branding, product development and fresh channels to market is impressive and why we have included this story. Gould has also attracted funding from an innovative venture capital group, LocalGlobe, that has enabled her to continue to develop her brand; the style and aesthetic of LocalGlobe fits perfectly with Soda's ethos.

We'll look at how to go about fundraising and what to expect from a venture capital fund in the next chapter.

References and useful resources

Further reading

Evans, P (2018) Tech plugs into high street, *The Times* [online]. Available at: https://www.thetimes.co.uk/article/tech-plugs-into-high-street-b9j7dwjxf

Websites

https://localglobe.vc/
https://www.radley.co.uk/
https://www.fashercise.com/

https://sophiehulme.com
https://www.lineapelle-fair.it/en/lineapelle
https://sodasays.co.uk/

Useful resources

https://analytics.google.com/analytics/web/provision/?authuser=0#/
    provision
https://plus.google.com/u/2/b/100805939335942634464/+A2zesolutionsforyou/
https://www.google.com/maps
https://www.google.com/business/
https://maps.google.com/localguides/signup
https://www.gov.uk/data-protection-your-business
https://reaper.com/
We Are Social Media – http://wersm.com
3 Social Media Books Everyone Should Read This October – http://bit.
    ly/2dd79Ys
Hootsuite Twitter feed – www.twitter.com/hootsuite
Grow your blog the right way – https://missinglettr.com/
Instagram Post Ideas: 6 Types of Content That Work – http://bit.ly/2eadFBd
Daily Hashtags Explained: What They Mean and How to Use Them –
    http://bit.ly/2e2aoTY
https://www.youtube.com/yt/about/press/
20+ Social Media Hacks and Tips From the Pros – http://bit.ly/2dljtJh
All of the Social Media Metrics That Matter – http://bit.ly/2dKjaZk
How to Find the Best Twitter Hashtags – http://bit.ly/2dN8FqD
Social Media Tips – http://huff.to/2dSPF6E
https://www.slideshare.net/
http://bit.ly/2e6rgO7

Part Three
Effective Finance Planning and Control

How to kickstart 09 your retail business

Key points

Make informed initial decisions about how you will run your business

Initiate good relations with the people, including the bank, you'll be working with

Be realistic about your start-up costs

Starting your business and selecting a structure

Maintaining a healthy balance sheet is critical for any successful business and achieving this takes planning and forecasting. Over the next few chapters in this book, we will look at:

- building a business plan;
- cash management;
- monitoring sales;
- helping your business to stay in a positive financial position.

The strategies we set out here have been developed by the authors; we've spent our careers in retail and we want to give start-up and independent retailers the skills and knowledge to run an efficient and successful business. The sector is ever-changing; as a retailer, you should expect to constantly work to improve your business and develop your retail skills. You should expect trading conditions to remain hard and very competitive. It is crucial that you fully understand how your business is operating against projections and what changes you can make to not only survive but grow it. It is essential you plan time to assess your financial position regularly and to respond to challenges as they reveal themselves. You might also find this course of action will throw up some additional opportunities.

But, to begin with the basics, we need first to look at starting your business. Making the right initial choices about your business structure, your bank, your VAT registration scheme and your employment obligations is very important. In terms of business structure, there are three main types to choose from:

- operate as a sole trader;
- form a business partnership;
- set up a limited company.

Sole trader

By opting for the sole trader route, you and your business are effectively one and the same, from both a tax and legal perspective. This means that you are personally responsible for the business and any debts it incurs. The profits you make, which are sales minus costs, are declared on your annual self-assessment tax return and classed as your personal income that year, even if it is not paid out as salary or into your personal bank account. You must pay income tax and national insurance on this at the standard income tax rates. While you do not need to register the business as such, you should tell the appropriate government department (in the UK, HM Revenue and Customs) that you are in operation and self-employed for tax purposes.

Business partnership

A partnership arrangement is similar to that of a sole trader, but differs in that it has more than one owner. All partners own a specified percentage of the profits, and the liabilities, so they must pay tax on that percentage. As with a sole trader, each partner's share of the profits is treated as their income.

Limited company

In the case of a limited company, the business becomes a separate legal entity. This means that the company must be formed, or incorporated, and registered appropriately (in the case of the UK, this is Companies House). It will also need to have certain standard legal documents that govern what it can do and what area of business it operates in. The company will be owned and controlled by those who own its shares and you can allocate shares to any number of people when the company is incorporated. You could keep all the shares for yourself, allocate some to a spouse, or sell them ('equity') to raise funds. There are advantages as well as extra administration duties attached to running a limited company.

Choosing a bank, fundraising, VAT and addressing costs

Once you have made your decision on your business structure, there are other practical, financial matters to attend to. Choose your bank wisely as it will play a major part in the success of your business. Not only do you want good service at a reasonable price, but you want to work with an organization that understands your business vision and will provide useful help and advice. Shop around, never exaggerate growth potential and always attend meetings with a full suite of documents.

The document folder you take to the bank should be presented in a file with eight sections and a contents page at the front. Each section should be clearly set out and you should aim to leave no questions unanswered. You may be asked to leave this folder with the bank, so be sure you have made copies before you go the meeting.

The documents you should take along to your bank meeting are listed below.

Checklist

✓ About you: your background and a CV

✓ Your business vision

✓ Where you intend to trade (physical store, online shop, or both)

✓ Why you think your business vision will work

✓ Your three-year plan

✓ Your cash requirement

✓ What you need that cash for – in detail

✓ What type of business structure you have selected

You should then fully investigate the various VAT registrations schemes that you may use; you may want to ask your accountant or lawyer for their advice on the best option for your business.

If you intend to employ people, you will need to register as an employer with HMRC. It's not well known, and worth noting here, that even if you expect your sales in the early years to fall below the VAT threshold, it is still possible to register for VAT and to reclaim the VAT you have been charged by suppliers and contractors.

Before you commence trading, you must ensure that you have the correct insurance in place. You can find an authorized insurer on the British Insurance Brokers' Association (BIBA) website. Finally, depending on the type of business you are running, you may need a specific licence or permit; you can check this on the gov.uk website.

When you initially start your business, no matter how detailed your projections, you will not be able to calculate exactly all your costs. Unexpected expenses will always arise. You will have to use your best estimate for a number of costs, such as heating and lighting, marketing, promotions, travel, printing and stationery. You can browse online to obtain ballpark quotes and source information on the suppliers available to you.

You should aim to keep your fixed overheads to a minimum, in case your turnover decreases. Review your overheads on a regular basis, working closely with your suppliers and landlord, if you have one. Remember, openness, transparency and honesty is the only way to work together – and taking them into your confidence will benefit you if you need them to offer some flexibility.

Preparing for a fundraising 'pitch' – be aware of investors' golden rules

Before any investor puts cash to work, they have to know what they are investing in. This might seem obvious, but too many proposals are vague and not properly thought through. Having a clear and well-presented plan means investors can condition themselves in terms of estimating when they might be able to realize a return and calculate whether an investment in your business satisfies their appetite for risk.

An investor will never invest in a proposition they don't immediately understand (just like today's customers) and can't be described on one sheet of paper. They will also do their own research, so never make unsubstantiated claims, never exaggerate, never make over-optimistic assumptions and never state 'facts' that can be easily checked.

Before you approach an investor, do your own due diligence on them. No investor will put all their eggs in one basket so avoid those where your business type overlaps with too many other businesses that they have invested in. Good and imaginative investors will go against the herd. If your proposition brings something fresh to the market, the more likely it will find funding. To get the best returns, an investor will ignore what everyone else is talking about and attempt to pick out an original concept.

As discussed later in this book, cash really is king to the investor. Dressing up a P&L account means nothing to an investor – it's the cash flow document that they will focus on. If your business demonstrates that it has the capability to generate cash, the chances of attracting an investor will dramatically improve.

Investors look out for businesses that possess the potential to realize pricing power. Pricing power is your ability to market your goods and services at prices that are both competitive and cannot be challenged by other retailers. Ted Baker has pricing power, Uniqlo has pricing power, Primark has pricing power, Burberry has pricing power, Zara has pricing power, Next has pricing power, Apple has pricing power, and Microsoft has pricing power. What these brands have in common is that everything they sell is sold and marketed under their own branded label.

Investors look for value and are not influenced solely by price. Just as a consumer does, they identify value, not just by the price, but by the quality, the uniqueness of the proposition and a sense that the business has the ability to continue to innovate.

CASE STUDY   Paul Smith

Paul Smith's first love was cycling, but, after crashing his bike and injuring himself, the man with a fresh vision opened a tiny funky fashion shop in Nottingham in 1970. He had looked around the menswear market at that time and could not find a look he admired or aspired to, anything that matched his fashion outlook. So, in an early example of what was to come from this driven man, he filled the gap he had identified. What impresses us is how Smith has gone on from those early beginnings to continually meet the needs of his target market without ever compromising his unique proposition.

He established a distinct handwriting very early on in his brand's development by designing a multicoloured cluster of stripes that he used in many ways – in his clothes collections, leather goods, stationery, fragrances and packaging. The signature stripe protected Smith's margin by removing 'identifiable brand price-cutting' by his competitors and helped to build his unique brand identity.

His collections expanded fast and his womenswear range was wonderfully received from its launch.

A good brand can be recognized before a label is seen and Smith has mastered this in a quirky, original way. His aesthetic travelled from shop to online to social media. His focus and confidence was brilliantly employed when he decided to present his collections personally at trade fairs and on export trips. Smith produces nothing; everything he sells in stores, online or wholesale is manufactured by very carefully selected licensees.

Paul Smith's primary export focus was Japan. Japanese businesses and consumers demand absolute perfection and Smith realized early on that meeting that challenge would benefit the standards in his entire business. He is admired hugely in Japan because he has studied the market and has respected both the standards and innovation demanded by the customer base.

Paul Smith's standards have never dropped and he has managed to avoid all of the missteps many world-renowned brands have experienced through compromising with below-standard factories. In short, Paul Smith is a terrific example of what we espouse in this book: vision, focus, control, belief, individuality, visibility, market awareness, customer respect and a relentless search for quality and differentiation.

References and useful resources

Websites

https://www.biba.org.uk/
https://trends.google.com/trends/
https://www.paulsmith.com/uk

Generating a results-driven business plan

10

Key points

A carefully made business plan will be your road map

Plan for hard as well as good times

Use spreadsheets to record and forecast your financials

The business plan and control

The business plan is comprised of a suite of documents. It does not 'die' or get put in a drawer when the business begins to trade. It is initially built on your market research, your vision and, of course, your assumptions. It must be dynamic because once trading starts you will measure your performance against your assumptions and make adjustments. You will have forecast sales and margins and, depending on achieving those two key metrics, will have planned to spend money on stock and commit to costs. If, after three months, a significant variation against your original assumptions, positive or negative, begins to emerge, you will need to make adjustments. These adjustments may result in needing to buy more to address a shortage of stock, may demand a look at margin as the gross profit line is looking weak, may require a review of costs that are running higher than expected, or cancelling stock because sales are lower than forecast. Every business from the very largest to the tiniest monitor their business in this way. If you pilot an aircraft and you can see a thunderstorm ahead on your radar, you take evasive action. Running a business requires the same forensic concentration on controls.

The vision

The business plan should begin with your idea and vision. Laura Jane Balance, co-founder of Merge Records, underlines this by saying, 'A retailer is a creative person who tries to craft something that appeals to other people. A retailer needs to be creative, observant, brave and patient.' Your retail business plan includes a short description of the industry and explains why you think you can penetrate the niche you want to trade in. When describing the particular industry, discuss the present outlook as well as future possibilities.

The market

You should also provide information on all the various markets and segments within the retail industry, including any new products or developments that will benefit or might adversely affect your business. A thorough market analysis forces you, the entrepreneur, to become familiar with all aspects of the market so that the target market can be defined and the company can be positioned in order to take its market share.

The competition and SWOT analysis

The purpose of the competitive analysis, sometimes referred to as a SWOT analysis and as we discussed in Chapter 3, is in the document to illustrate the strengths and weaknesses you perceive of the competitors within your market, strategies that will provide you with a distinct advantage, the steps you develop to prevent the competition from penetrating your market so you retain your unique proposition, and any weaknesses that can be exploited within the product development cycle.

The product

Your business plan should then include a section describing the product. This should cover how it will be sourced, purchased and produced, as well as if you intend to manufacture. Next, think about how the company will be marketed and the budget to deliver the marketing, including the social media and PR strategy, which needs to be clear and fully cost-estimated.

The controls

The control of operations together with a management plan is designed to describe just how the business will function on a daily basis. The operations plan will highlight the logistics of the organization such as the various responsibilities of the management team (if people are to be employed or involved), the tasks assigned to each person, and the capital and expense requirements related to the operations of the business.

The financial pack

A financial details section should include the profit and loss account, as well as a sensitivity analysis that illustrates the impact on the bottom line of turnover and margin swings, the cash flow forecast and the balance sheet (these will be covered in more detail later on in this chapter). These are always placed at the back of the business plan. But this doesn't mean these very important documents are any less important than the up-front material.

Financial planning and internal controls are vital to the survival and success of every retail business in today's market, especially the start-up. Driving sales, control and the measuring of stock, and managing the cash are only possible with effective internal controls and good financial planning. Retail start-ups have to accept that internal controls are something they should be responsible for and not leave that function to an accountant. Internal controls ensure financial information is accurate so the business can take appropriate action to ensure the business meets its objectives and goals, while protecting its assets (stock), managing cash and minimizing risk. Without adequate financial planning and internal controls, a retail business can very quickly spiral out of control as the investment in stock is high and management of cash flow vital.

The constituent parts of a business plan checklist

✓ The business's idea and vision

✓ The market

✓ The competition and SWOT analysis

✓ The product

✓ The controls

✓ The financial pack

Business plan layouts can vary and it takes time to produce a thorough business plan. If this is the first time you have attempted to put one together, there are a number of websites that can help you. You may find it helpful to ask a trusted friend, family member or colleague to help you brainstorm some of the checklist headings. Once you start to put your thoughts on paper, the reality of the business comes to life – really challenge yourself and put as much detail into the plan as possible. The business plan will be essential to obtain bank finance or investment, and going forward, the business plan will be your 'bible' to ensure that you are trading as you projected. It should enable you to react quickly to any variances, remove nasty surprises and give total visibility of your business. For a detailed checklist of things to include in your business plan, see the end of this chapter.

Financial planning for your business plan

Good financial planning is crucial in order for any business to be profitable. You need to take time out to monitor your money and plan for the future. Producing a business plan is your first step towards running a successful business. It's a summary of activity, which outlines how you will allocate resources, focus on key issues, and prepare for problems and opportunities. Your business plan is like a road map: if you don't know where you are heading, how do you know when you get there?

Break-even point

Your break-even point is when the money coming in equals the amount of money going out (including sales tax). To break-even, you need to make sure that you are able to make enough money to cover your costs. Always keep in mind the question of how low you can allow sales to go before your business turns to a net loss. Produce a plan with a 5 per cent decrease in sales, for example, and project how this would affect your profit and cash flow.

Financial details

As mentioned earlier in this chapter, your business plan should include a profit and loss account, a balance sheet and a cash flow forecast.

The profit and loss account summarizes the revenue or income coming into your business, and the costs, expenses or overheads, excluding VAT or sales tax, where applicable, over a specific period of your choice and will illustrate the money it takes to run your business profitably.

The balance sheet shows what the company owns (its assets), what it owes (its liabilities) and what has been invested (shareholders' equity). This is often shown as the following equation: Assets = liabilities + shareholders' equity.

The cash flow account in the business plan records the amounts of cash and cash equivalents entering and leaving the business, including VAT or sales tax, where applicable. This is a most important document since it allows you to predict the amount of cash you will have in the bank in the future, say three months out. You may have a big bill to pay in three months and a well-run cash flow forecast document will advise you in advance whether you will have the required funds. And it's better to know sooner rather than later so you can make plans.

Example spreadsheets

Our example spreadsheets and methodology illustrate all the financial reports that you should consider, including suggested expenditure headings for the cash flow document. If you don't have a clear understanding of financial terms and spreadsheets, you may find it helpful to source a mentor or accountant. The featured spreadsheets are examples only. With the support of an accountant or mentor, you can tailor them specifically for your business. Use each spreadsheet's supporting methodology as a template to apply to your business model.

To download copies of the full spreadsheets in a format you can use yourself, go to www.koganpage.com/retail-startup.

The Forecast Profit and Loss Account sample spreadsheet shows whether a business has generated profits, or sustained losses, during a specified period. Profits are essential to the long-term survival of a business and are an important source of funds for further investment. The profit figure may well be used by owners to measure the performance of the business and provide a value for the business.

Use the Forecast Profit and Loss Account example as a template – enter into a spreadsheet all the headers for your business and include all revenue, income, costs, expenses and overheads. You will then be able to calculate your gross margin as well as your profit and loss total for the year.

The Forecast Balance Sheet example spreadsheet gives a snapshot of the overall financial position of a business at a particular date. A balance sheet includes the assets, liabilities and equity of the company. It gives a statement of assets (things owned by the business) and liabilities (claims on the business) at that date. Maintaining a healthy balance sheet is critical for any successful business so it should clearly

Figure 10.1 Forecast profit and loss account

Profit and loss account		Jan	%	Jan	Feb	Mar	Apr	May	Jun
Original selling price, including VAT	A	326,429		80,000	35,000	45,000	45,000	50,000	71,429
Markdowns, including VAT		61,429		40,000	0	0	0	0	21,429
Markdowns (%)		50.00%		50.00%	0.00%	0.00%	0.00%	0.00%	30.00%
Total net sales, including VAT (SPTI)		265,000		40,000	35,000	45,000	45,000	50,000	50,000
Original selling price, excluding VAT	B	272,024		66,667	29,167	37,500	37,500	41,667	59,524
Markdowns, excluding VAT		51,190		33,333	0	0	0	0	17,857
Markdowns (%)		50.00%		50.00%	0.00%	0.00%	0.00%	0.00%	30.00%
Total net sales, excluding VAT (SPTE)	C	220,833	100.0	33,333	29,167	37,500	37,500	41,667	41,667
Opening stock	D	0	0.0	0	37,500	37,500	37,500	37,500	37,500
Purchases		137,637	55.0	61,833	10,792	13,875	13,875	15,417	21,845
Transfers to/from other divisions		0	0.0	0	0	0	0	0	0
Discounts on stock purchases		0	0.0						
Duty		0	0.0	0	0	0	0	0	0
Importation freight		0	0.0	0	0	0	0	0	0
Cost of goods sold	E	97,929	45.0	24,000	10,500	13,500	13,500	15,000	21,429
Stock provision/shrinkage	F	2,208	1.0	333	292	375	375	417	417
Closing stock	G	37,500	9.0	37,500	37,500	37,500	37,500	37,500	37,500
First gross margin	H	120,696	54.0	9,000	18,375	23,625	23,625	26,250	19,821

(continued)

Figure 10.1 (Continued)

Profit and loss account	Jan	%	Jan	Feb	Mar	Apr	May	Jun
Rent – Base	17,500	8.4	2,917	2,917	2,917	2,917	2,917	2,917
Rent – Turnover	0	0.0	0	0	0	0	0	0
Rent – Contribution/free period	-5,833	-1.4	-2,917	-2,917	0	0	0	0
Business rates	8,225	3.9	1,371	1,371	1,371	1,371	1,371	1,371
Water rates	125	0.1	21	21	21	21	21	21
Service charges	300	0.1	50	50	50	50	50	50
Light and heat	3,000	1.4	500	500	500	500	500	500
Maintenance/repairs – Building	600	0.3	100	100	100	100	100	100
Security	1,000	0.5	167	167	167	167	167	167
Landlords/building insurance	1,200	0.6	200	200	200	200	200	200
Total fixed overheads	26,117	13.9	2,408	2,408	5,325	5,325	5,325	5,325
Second gross margin	**94,580**	**40.1**	**6,592**	**15,967**	**18,300**	**18,300**	**20,925**	**14,496**
Salaries and pensions	25,000	12.0	4,167	4,167	4,167	4,167	4,167	4,167
National Insurance	3,200	1.5	533	533	533	533	533	533
Point of sale material	0	0.0	0	0	0	0	0	0
Marketing/public relations	5,000	2.4	833	833	833	833	833	833
Telephone/fax	1,500	0.7	250	250	250	250	250	250
Website/internet/email	0	0.0	0	0	0	0	0	0
Distribution/logistic costs	0	0.0	0	0	0	0	0	0
Printing/stationery	200	0.1	33	33	33	33	33	33
Supplies	2,500	1.2	417	417	417	417	417	417

			%						
	Postage/courier	500	0.2	83	83	83	83	83	83
	Subscriptions	0	0.0	0	0	0	0	0	0
	Professional costs	1,350	0.6	225	225	225	225	225	225
	Consultancy – Accounting	500	0.2	83	83	83	83	83	83
	Consultancy – Others	0	0.0	0	0	0	0	0	0
	Staff training/staff recruitment	0	0.0	0	0	0	0	0	0
	Audit/taxation	500	0.2	83	83	83	83	83	83
	Travel motor expenses	1,250	0.6	208	208	208	208	208	208
	Entertaining	0	0.0	0	0	0	0	0	0
	Cleaning	250	0.1	42	42	42	42	42	42
	Staff welfare	300	0.1	50	50	50	50	50	50
	Repairs – Product	1,200	0.6	200	200	200	200	200	200
	Sundry expenses	0	0.0	0	0	0	0	0	0
	Sundry income	0	0.0	0	0	0	0	0	0
	Lease costs	0	0.0	0	0	0	0	0	0
	Bank charges	0	0.0	0	0	0	0	0	0
	Interest payable	0	0.0	0	0	0	0	0	0
	Interest receivable	0	0.0	0	0	0	0	0	0
	Credit card charges	3,975	1.8	600	525	675	675	750	750
	Discounts allowed/till differences	120	0.1	20	20	20	20	20	20
	Exchange rate variances	0	0.0	0	0	0	0	0	0
	Depreciation/amortization	6,250	3.0	1,042	1,042	1,042	1,042	1,042	1,042
K	Total variable overheads	53,595	25.6	8,870	8,795	8,945	8,945	9,020	9,020
L	**Profit/(loss) before corporation tax**	**40,985**	**14.4**	**-2,278**	**7,172**	**9,355**	**9,355**	**11,905**	**5,476**
	Corporation tax	**0**	2.9						
	Profit/(loss) after corporation tax	**40,985**	11.6	**-2,278**	**7,172**	**9,355**	**9,355**	**11,905**	**5,476**

(continued)

Figure 10.1 (Continued)

Profit and loss account	Jan	%	Jan	Feb	Mar	Apr	May	Jun
Actual GP % total net sales SPTE (after m/d)	28.00		28.00	64.00	64.00	64.00	64.00	48.57
Actual GP % original selling price SPTI	70.00		70.00	70.00	70.00	70.00	70.00	70.00
Actual GP % original selling price SPTE	64.00		64.00	64.00	64.00	64.00	64.00	64.00

		Jan
Original selling price, including VAT (A) at 20%		326,429
Divide by 1.2		1.2
Equals original selling price, excluding VAT (B)	=	272,024
Cost of goods sold (E)		97,929
Plus stock provision/shrinkage (F)	+	2,208
Plus closing stock (G)	+	37,500
Equals purchases (D)	=	137,637
Total net sales, excluding VAT (C) is		220,833
Minus cost of goods sold (E)	–	97,929
Minus stock provision/shrinkage (F)	–	2,208
Equals first gross margin (H)	=	120,696

		Jun
First gross margin (H)		120,696
Minus total fixed overheads (I)	–	26,117
Equals second gross margin (J)	=	94,580
Second gross margin (J)		94,580
Minus total variable overheads (K)	–	53,595
Equals profit/(loss) before Corporation tax (L)	=	40,985

Figure 10.2 Forecast balance sheet

Balance sheet		31 Dec	31 Jan	28 Feb	31 Mar	30 Apr	31 May	30 Jun
Fixtures and fittings – Additions		0	50,000	0	0	0	0	0
Fixtures and fittings – Depreciation			1,042	1,042	1,042	1,042	1,042	1,042
Fixed assets	A	0	48,958	47,917	46,875	45,833	44,792	43,750
Stock			37,500	37,500	37,500	37,500	37,500	37,500
Debtors – Shop takings			2,000	1,750	2,250	2,250	2,500	2,500
Debtors – Others								
Rent deposits/guarantees			0	0	0	0	0	0
VAT			3,915	0	0	0	0	0
Corporation tax								
Cash in hand			0	0	0	0	0	0
Cash at bank			0	0	0	0	0	0
Prepayments			0	0	0	0	0	0
Current assets	B	0	43,415	39,250	39,750	39,750	40,000	40,000
Net current assets	C	0	–51,136	–42,923	–32,527	–22,130	–9,183	–2,665
Trade creditors – Stock		0	61,833	10,792	13,875	13,875	15,417	21,845
Trade creditors – Rent		0	0	0	–7,000	–3,500	–0	–7,000
Trade creditors – Overheads		0	2,930	2,990	2,870	2,930	2,990	2,870
Loan 1		0	0	0	0	0	0	0
Loan 2		0	0	0	0	0	0	0
Loan 3		0	0	0	0	0	0	0

Figure 10.2 (Continued)

Balance sheet		31 Dec	31 Jan	28 Feb	31 Mar	30 Apr	31 May	30 Jun
PAYE and National Insurance		0	1,532	1,532	1,532	1,532	1,532	1,532
VAT		0	0	1,337	7,672	6,335	13,503	20,672
Corporation tax		0	0	0	0	0	0	0
Bank overdraft		0	28,256	65,523	53,328	40,708	15,741	2,746
Accrued expenses		0						
Current liabilities	D	**0**	**94,551**	**82,173**	**72,277**	**61,880**	**49,183**	**42,665**
Total assets less liabilities	E	**0**	**-2,178**	**4,993**	**14,348**	**23,703**	**35,608**	**41,085**
Share capital		0	100	100	100	100	100	100
Reserves brought forward		0	0	0	0	0	0	0
Profit for year		0	-2,278	4,893	14,248	23,603	35,508	40,985
Shareholders' equity	F	**0**	**-2,178**	**4,993**	**14,348**	**23,703**	**35,608**	**41,085**

Using figures for 31 Jan:

Fixed Assets (A) = £50,000 minus Depreciation £1,042 = £48,958

Current Assets (B) = £43,415 (adding up of Stock through to Prepayments)

Current Liabilities (D) = £94,551 (adding up of Trade creditors – Stock through to Accrued expenses)

Net Current Assets (C) = £-51,136 (Current Assets (B) £43,415 minus Current Liabilities (D) £94,551)

Total Assets Less Liabilities (E) = £-2,178 (Net Current Assets (C) £-51,136 plus Fixed Assets (A) £48,958)

Shareholders' Equity (Share Capital plus Reserves brought forward plus Profit for year) = (F) £-2,178

Figure 10.3 Forecast cash flow

Cash flow forecast		B/Fwd	Jan	Feb	Mar	Apr	May	Jun
Income								
	Shop receipts – same month		38,000	33,250	42,750	42,750	47,500	47,500
	Shop receipts – following month		0	2,000	1,750	2,250	2,250	2,500
	Share capital		100					
	Loan 1							
	Loan 2							
	Loan 3							
	Total income	A	38,100	35,250	44,500	45,000	49,750	50,000
Expenditure								
Excl VAT	Purchases – 7 days (100%)		0	0	0	0	0	0
Excl VAT	Purchases – 30 days (0%)			61,833	10,792	13,875	13,875	15,417
Excl VAT	Purchases – 60 days (0%)			0	0	0	0	0
Excl VAT	Purchases – discounts			0	0	0	0	0
Excl VAT	Duty			0	0	0	0	0
Excl VAT	Importation freight			0	0	0	0	0
Incl VAT	Rent – base		7,000		10,500			10,500
Incl VAT	Rent – turnover			0		0		
Incl VAT	Rent – contribution / free period		–7,000		0			
No VAT	Business rates		1,371	1,371	1,371	1,371	1,371	1,371
No VAT	Water rates		21	21	21	21	21	21
Incl VAT	Service charges				180			180
Incl VAT	Light and heat		600	600	600	600	600	600

(continued)

Figure 10.3 (Continued)

Cash flow forecast	B/Fwd	Jan	Feb	Mar	Apr	May	Jun
Incl VAT	Maintenance/repairs – Building			120	120	120	120	120
Incl VAT	Security			200	200	200	200	200
No VAT	Landlords/building insurance		200	200	200	200	200	200
No VAT	Salaries and pensions		3,168	3,168	3,168	3,168	3,168	3,168
No VAT	National Insurance							
Incl VAT	Point of sale material			0	0	0	0	0
Incl VAT	Marketing/public relations			1,000	1,000	1,000	1,000	1,000
Incl VAT	Telephone/fax			300	300	300	300	300
Incl VAT	Website/internet/email			0	0	0	0	0
Incl VAT	Distribution/logistic costs			0	0	0	0	0
Incl VAT	Printing/stationery		40	40	40	40	40	40
Incl VAT	Supplies			500	500	500	500	500
No VAT	Postage/courier		83	83	83	83	83	83
Incl VAT	Subscriptions			0	0	0	0	0
Incl VAT	Professional costs		270	270	270	270	270	270
No VAT	Consultancy – Accounting		83	83	83	83	83	83
Incl VAT	Consultancy – Others			0	0	0	0	0
Incl VAT	Staff training/staff recruitment			0	0	0	0	0
Incl VAT	Audit/taxation			100	100	100	100	100
Incl VAT	Travel/motor expenses		250	250	250	250	250	250
No VAT	Entertaining		0	0	0	0	0	0
Incl VAT	Cleaning			50	50	50	50	50
No VAT	Staff welfare		50	50	50	50	50	50
No VAT	Repairs – Product		200	200	200	200	200	200
Incl VAT	Sundry expenses			0	0	0	0	0

No VAT	Sundry income	0	0	0	0	0	0
Incl VAT	Lease costs						
No VAT	Bank charges	0	0	0	0	0	0
No VAT	Interest payable	0	0	0	0	0	0
No VAT	Interest receivable	0	0	0	0	0	0
No VAT	Credit card charges	600	525	675	675	750	750
No VAT	Discounts allowed/till differences	20	20	20	20	20	20
No VAT	Exchange rate variances	0	0	0	0	0	0
No VAT	Capital expenditure	60,000	0	0	0	0	0
Incl VAT	Corporation tax	0	0	0	0	0	0
No VAT	PAYE	1,532	1,532	1,532	1,532	1,532	1,532
	Rent deposit						
	Till float/cash in hand						
	Loan 1						
	Loan 2						
	Loan 3						
	VAT return	0	0	0	7,672	0	0
	Total expenditure B	66,356	72,517	32,305	32,380	24,783	37,005
	Monthly – Cash in hand/(Overdraft) C	−28,256	−37,267	12,195	12,620	24,967	12,995
	Cumulative – Cash in hand/(Overdraft) D	−28,256	−65,523	−53,328	−40,708	−15,741	−2,746

Using figures for Feb:

Total income (A)	35,250	Monthly – cash in hand/(overdraft) (C)
Minus total expenditure (B)	− 72,517	Plus cumulative – cash in hand/(overdraft)
Equals monthly – cash in hand/(overdraft) (C)	= −37,267	From previous month – Jan (D)
		Equals cumulative – cash in hand/(overdraft)
		For present month – Feb (D)

set out these points, at a given point of time of your choosing, normally from the end of January. This is your snapshot of the health of the company.

A balance sheet has two sides that must balance. Side one shows the fixed assets: fixtures, fittings, machines, depreciated assets; and current assets: stock, sales and VAT that have been collected. Side two sets out the businesses liabilities or financial obligations: unpaid-for stock, rent, business rates, PAYE and NI, bank charges and other expenses. To balance the sheet, current liabilities are deducted from current assets to arrive at total assets, minus liabilities. This total asset figure must match, or balance, the company's share capital (number of shares in circulation) plus the profit for the period (this is known as the equity). The sheet is now balanced. A great video on this topic can be viewed on YouTube, see references and further reading at the end of this chapter.

The Forecast Cash Flow sample spreadsheet records the amounts of cash and cash equivalents entering and leaving the business, summarizing a total expenditure figure. The total income monthly figure increases from January to December. This particular business trades seasonally because shop receipts are reduced in February and August, the periods after Christmas and the summer sale. We can see in Expenditure: Purchases – 30 days (0%) that the payment for the creditors' bill of £61,833 has left the business in February, resulting in a deficit figure at the end of the month. The overdraft facility is used to support the cash flow. As the creditors are paid over the year, we see the figures increasing again.

CASE STUDY   Emma J Shipley

Emma J Shipley is a wonderful start-up example of creating an idea, delivering a vision, exploiting her skills and executing it. Shipley launched her brand at London Fashion Week in 2012 after graduating from the Royal College of Art in London. She had the confidence and courage to begin a business rather than work for someone else. She sensibly followed the processes we explained earlier in this chapter and did not rush in, which often forces start-ups to backtrack.

Her first task was to put in place financial projections together with a business plan, with which she was helped by her father. As an award-winning graphic artist and designer specializing in fine drawing, Shipley spotted a gap in the market for her unique style and the subject matter she intended to focus on. She took inspiration from patterns in nature, with a surreal and magical twist. This became her unique selling proposition.

Shipley launched her label, focusing first on luxury printed scarves. They were spotted by Liberty of London – this was her break. The famous London-based boutique Browns followed. Shipley's strategy included a drive to collaborate with famous brands, such as the Disney Company. She realized that she could leverage her artistic skill, essentially licensing it, rather than investing large sums in manufacturing herself. This was a very intelligent approach for a start-up and it soon led to other collaborations, most recently wallpaper and furnishing fabrics.

Emma J Shipley creates truly original designs that sets her apart from her competitors. She began her business in exactly the right way: she had a vision to exploit her skill, studied the market, saw a gap, developed a financial plan, started slowly, kept her design discipline, marketed herself with a brilliant social media strategy and listened carefully to her closest advisors.

The business plan checklist

Executive summary

✓ Business intention – a description of what your business will do

✓ Business details – registered company name and contact details

✓ Business owner and staff details (include role and salary for each individual)

Vision

✓ The business idea (what you want to achieve)

✓ Brand identity (include the experience you intend to create, how you intend to give fantastic service, and your unique specialism)

✓ Business differentiation (competition)

✓ Business goals (include three-year plan)

✓ Measure the size of the market and identify the potential of your market share

✓ Show yourself to be an expert in your chosen field, but with a 'beginner's' mindset

Marketing

✓ Market research (trends and demand for your product or service)

✓ Customer profiles and behaviour (who are they and how do they shop?)

✓ Competitors (identify strengths and weaknesses (local, small, large, online))

✓ Market risks (risks identified and solution required)

✓ Pricing (consider how much customers are prepared to pay and compare with the competition)

✓ Recognize and understand your growth potential

✓ Promotions and events (how and where will you promote your product or service?)

Operating the business

✓ People costs (if you intend to employ)

✓ Premises and occupancy costs

✓ Suppliers (key suppliers and their credit terms)

✓ Equipment (fixtures and resources needed to operate)

✓ Operational risks (risks identified and solutions articulated)

Finance

✓ Start-up costs

✓ Sourcing finance

✓ Financial risks (risks identified and impact minimized)

✓ Profit and loss forecast

✓ Balance sheet

✓ Cash flow forecast

References and useful resources

Further reading

Ballance, L, Cook, J, McCaughan, M (2009) *Our Noise: The story of Merge Records, the indie label that got big and stayed small*, Algonquin Books, Chapel Hill, NC

Website

https://emmajshipley.com/

Useful resource

https://www.youtube.com/watch?v=ixCPM5HznRU

A straightforward guide to sales, stock and profit

> **Key points**
>
> Research your market and its potential
>
> Note the importance of balancing sales with costs
>
> Use data to keep an eye on the bottom line

Research the market to formulate your assumptions and projections

Collect all possible data that will make you an expert in your field and more aware of the customers that you're intending to sell to. You should be constantly aiming to be better informed about how these customers behave, what turns them on and how they might react to your products or services. By using openly available market research, such as that provided by the Oxford College of Marketing, you will also be able to identify and grow confident that the demographic target market you are focusing on is indeed the group that you believe will need and desire the product or service you are bringing to the market.

To help understand the market and the customer you are targeting, you should ask yourself the following questions:

- What market need does your business address?
- Which products serve that need?

- Where do your potential customers buy now?
- What demographic are you targeting for this service or product?
- What price band will they be prepared to shop in?
- Who are the principal competitors?
- Is your business or product something new and fresh with a unique selling point (USP)?
- Are there uncontrollable factors that might have an impact on customers' decisions (recession, changing trends, Brexit (UK)) that you may need to factor into your plans?
- Have you calculated the potential growth and demand in your chosen field?

Projections should be based on firm assumptions following research made into the market you intend selling to. Four factors to base your sales assumptions on are:

- the relevance of the products you are selling;
- the specific customer group you intend targeting;
- the price bands you choose to sell your products in;
- the resources you plan to use to sell effectively.

Forecast sales for your start-up must be based, as we have said, not only on very careful research, but also on your best-informed sense of how you expect your business will perform. Starting a business is exciting and risky, but that does not mean that forensic research and ongoing market due diligence should ever be glossed over. Once the business has begun, analyse sales week on week, month on month and believe what your figures and statistics are telling you.

Key metrics

The key measures below will tell you everything you need to know about the financial health, or otherwise, of your business. These metrics do not measure your vision, the stock you buy, the place in the market you have chosen to be in, or whether trading in a shop or online have been the correct choices. That is a combination of strategy and tactics. These metrics anticipate if the course you've adopted is moving in a profitable direction.

Key metrics

- Sales and gross profit
- Fixed overheads
- Variable expenses
- Capital expenditure (capex)
- Depreciation
- Cash

Sales and gross profit

Gross profit is also referred to as 'gross margin' and 'gross income'. It is the amount of money left from the sales revenue, after VAT or sales tax, is paid. After deducting the cost of sales, the cost of the product or service you are selling, what remains is the sum that the company has left to run the business. All expenses and overheads will be deducted from this figure.

Pricing will be one of the biggest decisions you make – and the gross profit will be the main financial factor contributing to the success or failure of your business. Most stock control systems monitor gross profit, but spreadsheets can easily be set up to give you the same information. Gross profit analysis is the simple and accurate way of checking whether sales are being made at the optimum selling price to retain your competitiveness and keep your business profitable.

The gross profit margin calculation example in Figure 11.1 demonstrates how gross profit margin (GPM) is calculated. You can see that if the cost price (that is, the price you pay to produce the goods and services you are selling) remains static, a retail price variation produces a different margin. Maintaining a good relationship with

Figure 11.1   Example of different gross profit margin calculations

Retail selling price including VAT	£50.00	£55.00	£60.00	£65.00	£70.00
Less VAT @ 20% on RSP excluding VAT	(£8.34)	(£9.17)	(£10.00)	(£10.84)	(£11.67)
Retail selling price excluding VAT	£41.67	£45.83	£50.00	£54.16	£58.33
Cost price	£12.50	£12.50	£12.50	£12.50	£12.50
Gross margin/profit	£29.17	£33.33	£37.50	£41.66	£45.83
Gross margin/profit %	70.00%	72.73%	75.00%	76.92%	78.57%
Retail selling price excluding VAT	£100,000	£100,000	£100,000	£100,000	£100,000
Gross margin/profit %	70.00%	72.73%	75.00%	76.92%	78.57%
Gross margin/profit	£69,999	£72,726	£74,999	£76,922	£78,571

suppliers may offer opportunities to purchase goods, at certain times of the year, at less than the usual cost price. This will add valuable points to your margin. Remember downward GPM movements, for example sale markdowns, will produce a dramatic effect on your bottom line.

Example spreadsheets

The example spreadsheets and methodology that appear in this chapter can be tailored specifically for your business. Use each spreadsheet's supporting methodology as a template to apply to your business model.

To download copies of the full spreadsheets in a format you can use yourself, go to www.koganpage.com/retail-startup.

Fixed overheads and variable expenses

There are two types of overhead expenses for any business: fixed and variable. Fixed overheads will not change with any fluctuation of your sales, but your variable overheads will. Fixed overheads are those that you need to pay even if you make no sales – this includes rent if you trade in a shop, rates, service charges, light, heat, power, building maintenance, loans and so on. You should always keep your fixed overheads to a minimum in case turnover decreases.

Referring to overheads as fixed suggests you have no control, but in fact you *do* have some control. Being transparent with your landlord and the local authority is the best way to operate and means you can discuss the rent and rate costs. Always explain the reasons if you feel that the combined costs may drive you out of business. Never accept a rent renewal without negotiation. We strongly recommend that, if you anticipate an increase in rent and if sales are struggling, send your landlord your monthly accounts three months ahead of the rent review date. As well as this, it's worth regularly challenging light, heat, power and water costs, and always challenge insurance companies at renewal time. In many cases, because the market is so competitive, you will achieve a reduction. If not, shop around.

Variable overheads include people costs – and this will be one of your biggest overheads. As well as salaries, you will also have the cost of National Insurance in the UK, pension contributions and welfare. So, managing variable costs means managing the people you employ; this includes considering part-time employment (especially if your turnover pattern is seasonal). Apart from the fixed costs mentioned earlier, people will be the biggest expenditure. So we suggest you set a percentage of people costs to sales in the P&L account and try very hard to stick to it. If that percentage creeps up, it is evident and you will need to act.

Variable costs means exactly that and you have complete control on what you spend. Whether it's people, marketing, PR, search engine optimization, website costs, point of sale material, travel, entertaining or professional costs, it's important you consider every penny spent.

The overhead expenses example in Figure 11.2 shows a number of fixed and variable overheads. The overhead categories will differ from business to business, so study the split between fixed and variable carefully. The total of these two overheads is deducted from the gross profit to reveal the net profit of the business before the deduction of corporation tax, should it be payable.

Figure 11.2 Example of fixed and variable overheads

Profit and loss account		Total	Jan	Feb	Mar	Apr	May	Jun
Rent – base		17,500	2,917	2,917	2,917	2,917	2,917	2,917
Rent – turnover		0	0	0	0	0	0	0
Rent – contribution/free period		-5,833	-2,917	-2,917	0	0	0	0
Business rates		8,225	1,371	1,371	1,371	1,371	1,371	1,371
Water rates		125	21	21	21	21	21	21
Service charges		300	50	50	50	50	50	50
Light and heat		3,000	500	500	500	500	500	500
Maintenance/repairs – building		600	100	100	100	100	100	100
Security		1,000	167	167	167	167	167	167
Landlords/building insurance		1,200	200	200	200	200	200	200
Total fixed overheads	A	26,117	2,408	2,408	5,325	5,325	5,325	5,325
Salaries and pensions		25,000	4,167	4,167	4,167	4,167	4,167	4,167
National Insurance		3,200	533	533	533	533	533	533
Point of sale material		0	0	0	0	0	0	0
Marketing/public relations		5,000	833	833	833	833	833	833
Telephone/fax		1,500	250	250	250	250	250	250
Website/internet/email		0	0	0	0	0	0	0
Distribution/logistic costs		0	0	0	0	0	0	0
Printing/stationery		200	33	33	33	33	33	33
Supplies		2,500	417	417	417	417	417	417
Postage/courier		500	83	83	83	83	83	83

Subscriptions	0	0	0	0	0	0	0
Professional costs	1,350	225	225	225	225	225	225
Consultancy – accounting	500	83	83	83	83	83	83
Consultancy – others	0	0	0	0	0	0	0
Staff training/staff recruitment	0	0	0	0	0	0	0
Audit/taxation	500	83	83	83	83	83	83
Travel motor expenses	1,250	208	208	208	208	208	208
Entertaining	0	0	0	0	0	0	0
Cleaning	250	42	42	42	42	42	42
Staff welfare	300	50	50	50	50	50	50
Repairs – product	1,200	200	200	200	200	200	200
Sundry expenses	0	0	0	0	0	0	0
Sundry income	0	0	0	0	0	0	0
Lease costs	0	0	0	0	0	0	0
Bank charges	0	0	0	0	0	0	0
Interest payable	0	0	0	0	0	0	0
Interest receivable	0	0	0	0	0	0	0
Credit card charges	3,975	600	525	675	675	750	750
Discounts allowed/till differences	120	20	20	20	20	20	20
Exchange rate variances	0	0	0	0	0	0	0
Depreciation/amortization	6,250	1,042	1,042	1,042	1,042	1,042	1,042
Total variable overheads **B**	53,595	8,870	8,795	8,945	8,945	9,020	9,020

(continued)

Figure 11.2 *(Conttinued)*

This spreadsheet shows the numerous elements that will make up your fixed and variable overheads.

The total of all the elements within Fixed overheads is shown in Total fixed overheads (A).

The total of all the elements within Variable overheads is shown in Total variable overheads (B).

Example:

Rent – base is	17,500
divided by 6 (months)	6
gives a monthly overhead of =	2,917

The net profit of the business before tax is what is known as the 'bottom line'. The bottom line, in positive territory, is everything you are working towards and the reason you are in business. It's the fundamental and most important factor that demonstrates, in black and white, that your efforts and vision have paid off. Although it's the total amount of money you have made (or lost) over a specific period, we want to stress the importance of maintaining your cash flow document as it is this document that explicitly gives you a warning of possible trouble ahead, so you can react. A retail business can be in loss for ten months of the year and only turn profitable in the last period, normally the Christmas period. A good retailer will work very hard to convert loss-making months to bring them to at least a break-even position. You will then see an end of year 'bottom line' to be proud of!

Capital expenditure

Capital expenditure, or capex, is the purchase of assets such as property, building works, fixtures and fittings, computers and office equipment. The expense is capitalized and shown in the balance sheet as a fixed asset and normally written off, also termed depreciated or amortized, over the useful life of the asset. For example, you may build a shop interior (with a ten-year lease), for £50,000. You would most likely depreciate or amortize this cost over ten years, charging £5,000 a year to the profit and loss account. This will lower profits but also lower any corporation tax liability. It is important to note that, although the charge to the profit and loss is only £5,000 a year, the initial cost of £50,000 will reduce your cash availability at the outset. You may want to consider separate finance for the purchase of fixed assets so as not to stretch the working capital of the business. Lease finance is a popular form of finance and all international banks have a lease finance partner. You should strictly adhere to your capex budget and don't spend more than you've allocated – these sums have a big impact on cash flow. Whenever you spend a large sum on a shop fit-out, essential building works, developing a transactional website or stock, ensure that there is a binding contract between you and the supplier/contractor. Insert a penalty charge for late completion of works and have an understanding that late deliveries may be cancelled by you. A late launch will mean lost sales, which cannot be recouped. Before you sign purchase orders, ask the manufacturers if they would be willing to supply the product over an agreed period of time (only if it suits you, of course). Most manufacturers are only too willing to feed in product and it helps you to spread your payments too.

Depreciation

The term 'depreciation' is used to represent a reduction in the value of an asset over its useful life, in particular due to 'wear and tear'. Depreciation occurs when a replacement is available that has more advantages over a current asset. For example, depreciation can be applied to computers, machinery, fixtures and fittings, light fittings, window mannequins, but not stock. These assets can be depreciated over a period of time, usually three years. Depreciating these assets is vital to the financial wellbeing of your company. If you have invested, say, £9,000 in a variety of assets, depreciating them over three years means that each year the business will deduct £3,000 from its profit or add to its losses*. After three years, if those 'written off' assets continue to have a useful life and do not need to be replaced, then the business will have reduced its operational costs because those assets need no longer be accounted for in the P&L. Depreciating over a short period is conservative and sensible. (*In its early years, if a business sustains losses – not unusual – those losses can be used to reduce corporation tax when the company begins to trade profitably.)

This spreadsheet example in Figure 11.3 demonstrates how to keep a record of your fixed assets and how to calculate your depreciation charge. The example shows that computer/office equipment is being depreciated over three years from the month of purchase, and shop fixtures and fittings over ten years. There are a number of ways and varying rates to depreciate your assets so a conversation with your accountant/auditor is advisable. Make sure you understand exactly what is being done in your name. When a fixed asset is acquired, it is expected to have a useful life, spanning a number of accounting

Figure 11.3 Example of a depreciation/amortization schedule

Nominal account:
Computer/office equipment
Depreciation period: 3 years – 33.33% per year

Date	Details		Additions/ Disposals	Depreciation B/Fwd	Depn Jan	Depn Feb	Depn Mar	Depn Apr	Depn May	Depn Jun
01.01.11	Computer	A	449.00	0.00	12.47	12.47	12.47	12.47	12.47	12.47
05.03.11	Fax machine	B	149.00	0.00			4.14	4.14	4.14	4.14
06.06.11	Desk	C	580.00	0.00						16.11
		D	**1,178.00**	0.00	12.47	12.47	16.61	16.61	16.61	32.72

Nominal account:
Fixtures and fittings
Depreciation period: 10 years – 10% per year

Date	Details		Additions/ Disposals	Depreciation B/Fwd	Depn Jan	Depn Feb	Depn Mar	Depn Apr	Depn May	Depn Jun
01.01.11	Shop fit-out	E	50,000.00	0.00	416.67	416.67	416.67	416.67	416.67	416.67
05.01.11	Alarm	F	1,200.00	0.00	10.00	10.00	10.00	10.00	10.00	10.00
04.04.11	Fixtures	G	5,000.00	0.00				41.67	41.67	41.67
09.09.11	Extra lighting	H	2,000.00	0.00						
	Total	I	**58,200.00**	0.00	426.67	426.67	426.67	468.33	468.33	468.33

Total Additions – Cash   59,378.00 Annual depreciation charge to P&L   5,865.47   **5,865.47**

(continued)

Figure 11.3 (*Continued*)

When a fixed asset is aquired, it is expected to have a useful life spanning a number of accounting periods. It would therefore be inappropriate to charge the cost of its acquisition to any single accounting period. If this was done, the resulting profit/loss figure would understate performance for that period. In subsequent periods, however, profits would be overstated. Depreciation charges the cost of an asset over its expected useful life. It will appear as one of the expenses in the profit and loss account.

Rows A, B, C, E, F, G, and H are various assets purchased.

A+B+C = D

E+F+G+H = I

Example 1

    (A) divided by 100 × 33.33 (3 years, 33.33% per year) = £149.65 (total depreciation for 12 months)

    £149.65 divided by 12 (ie over 12 months) = £12.47 per month

Example 2

    (E) divided by 100 × 10 (10 years, 10% per year) = £5,000 (total depreciation for 12 months)

    £5,000 divided by 12 (ie over 12 months) = £416.67 per month

periods. This is the correct and conservative approach. It would therefore be inappropriate to charge or depreciate the cost of this acquisition to any single accounting period. If this were to be done, the resulting profit/loss figure would understate performance for that period and overstate profits in subsequent periods.

Banks and cash management

You should open only one business account and it should not be connected in any way to your personal affairs. If possible, and we strongly recommend this, the account should be opened in a different bank from the one you use personally or even have family connections with. The reason for this is that we have seen too many examples of banks drawing on private accounts, in error, and confusing business affairs with private affairs. When you begin a new enterprise and begin a new relationship with a bank, expect to be respected, to be taken seriously and to have clearly explained to you all the services, including digital services, the bank can and will offer.

Banks today encourage small businesses and you should expect to be listened to carefully when you present your business plan. Be clear at the outset whether you want an overdraft facility and if, as a result, you are required to sign a personal guarantee, make absolutely sure it is capped at a figure you can afford to lose. We have seen too many cases of people having to take out second mortgages or even selling their homes because they did not cap the personal guarantee at the bank. You will say at the time you open an account that you will never exceed your overdraft facility. There will be cases when you simply can't avoid this due to issues beyond your control. For example, a supplier going bust just after you have paid an invoice, but before the goods are in – you will need to replace this merchandise. Or, say, the road you trade in suffers a burst water main and you're flooded out – trade will be disrupted for weeks and sales will crash. Provided you communicate immediately with your bank and explain clearly what has occurred they are likely to accommodate you. Banks hate surprises. Especially nasty surprises.

You have every right to expect an honest, speedy and direct response to your proposition and not be moved around the organization. This wastes your valuable time and will hold you up. We are aware that relationship managers in banks frequently move and when they do they often fail to inform you of who will take over. When you do know, make an appointment to visit the bank and go over everything with the new person. It's tiresome, but vital and you should make it clear at the outset that you expect to connect regularly with the bank and absolutely expect to be kept informed of any management changes.

Internet banking will give your cash management complete transparency and is the cheapest method of banking. Viewing your business account should be the first job on your list each and every day so you know who has paid you and what funds are available to pay your bills. No matter how successful your latest sales push has been, or how much profit you have made, nothing brings you down as effectively as a cash flow crisis. In order to keep certain fundamentals of your business running smoothly, set up standing orders or direct debits for your regular utility bills and business rates that you can pay over twelve months, interest free. We would recommend resisting direct debits or standing orders on stock.

Open and honest negotiations of credit terms with your goods suppliers, landlord, local authority and power companies are required at the outset and need to be reviewed constantly as your business grows. Make sure that the terms you have agreed are possible to achieve, as you will find it harder to renegotiate if you have defaulted in any way – and always speak to your creditors if you foresee a problem. Don't give credit, even if you have made stringent checks on the relevant party to ensure that there is no risk of a bad debt. It's rare for a new business to give credit, but it can occur if you do not always hold everything in stock. A good customer may want you to order in an expensive item or a selection of items you don't normally stock. You agree, you order the items and then the customer changes their mind. This is embarrassing and costly to you. If you are prepared to do this, ask for 75 per cent of the full retail price upfront.

Related issues to consider after three months of operation

Three months may not seem like a long enough period to judge how your new business is performing. You have probably put in months even years of work, research and mental preparation before the doors are open or the website launched. You have become so close to, and rightly so in love with, what you have created that hopes and optimism crowd out every other emotion. As we say in this book, consumers today make instantaneous decisions and will have quickly made their judgments on your enterprise. You will only receive their honest opinions by seeing the business they are giving you in hard cash terms.

That's why three months in is a good to time to take the temperature of your business and to look closely at all the measures we have discussed in this book. The key measure after three months of operation is the cash in bank. If your cash is where you predicted it would be, that's excellent. The key point here is that you have to get into a very regular routine of cash monitoring. Imagine if, instead of stock, your shop floor or office was stacked with bundles of cash. You rightly would be quite sensitive about this. Well, the stock you have together with everything else was paid for with cash to get the business off the ground, so it must be watched equally as carefully. Three months of trading will reveal so much. Sales performance, margins achieved, stock intake, actual variable costs, all set against the assumptions in your plan. The cash figure we mentioned is the measure, but it's how it got there that is so interesting. It is quite possible that you need do nothing at all, which is reassuring – and a terrific result. But you may need to adjust something, and it's better done now than after six months of operations. We can assure you that monitoring of this type goes on in the mightiest of concerns, so please do follow our suggestions.

Checklist

Products you are selling

- ✓ Do you have a new line to introduce?
- ✓ How did your products perform month on month?
- ✓ Are there trends emerging that could improve performance?
- ✓ Can you predict certain lines that will sell fast?
- ✓ Do you foresee a drop in sales due to competition on certain products?

Customers you are selling to

- ✓ Do you anticipate an increase in footfall and site visits?
- ✓ Are you increasing your marketing and social media activity?
- ✓ Are you increasing promotions or improving your merchandising?
- ✓ Have you identified physical and online hot spots?
- ✓ Are you aware of the average transaction value (ATV)?
- ✓ Is ATV growing or declining?
- ✓ Are you tracking returning customers?
- ✓ Do you have sufficient resource to meet demand?

The prices you intend to sell at

- ✓ Have you had to reduce some prices or are your prices competitive?
- ✓ Are margins stable?
- ✓ If you have a net margin objective, how much mark-up do you need to apply?
- ✓ Do you have different margin objectives for different products?
- ✓ Do you measure net margin daily/weekly?
- ✓ Do you measure net margin on all sales and by product group?
- ✓ If VAT is applicable to your product, have you ensured you have factored it in?
- ✓ Do you require a solicitor to check your Conditions of Sale for your online sales?

What we have noted in this checklist is a linked, three-part 'health check', similar to checking your heart rate after a 10-km run or an airline pilot going through a pre-flight take-off check. You are checking yourself, your assumptions, and relying on no one else. You are giving yourself the promise that you intend to run your business professionally and that you will continually measure the vital signs, and... keep an eagle eye on the cash.

References and useful resources

Reference

Oxford College of Marketing (27 Nov 2014) 'Why it's important to understand the customer's buying behaviour' [online]. Available at: https://blog.oxfordcollegeofmarketing.com/2014/11/27/why-its-important-to-understand-the-customers-buying-behaviour/

Website

www.experian.co.uk

Selection and management of retail systems and controls

12

Key points

Financial monitoring

Essential performance reports

Stock turn

Examine the numbers, closely

If you don't fully understand how your business is performing, you will not be able to decide what action is required and what your priorities should be. Producing reliable financial information will therefore play a big part in the success of your business and reliable information doesn't have to come from complex accounting systems. Initially, keep it simple and only move on to more sophisticated systems as your business grows.

If this is not your area of strength, try hard to seek financial support and expertise. Understand and monitor figures on a regular basis (daily, weekly, monthly and yearly) as this will help you to detect and anticipate problems before they arise. Early detection of money problems will allow you to take action quickly and make changes gradually rather than drastically. Total visibility is key to every successful business. You must be constantly aware of your cash position, whether or not you are able to pay bills on time and to see whether you are trading profitably. Reacting too late to a downturn trend in sales because you are failing to monitor the key financial pulses will make it very difficult to explain to suppliers why payments are going to be late. Your credibility will suffer, so be vigilant in anticipating problems by keeping track. As you move from planning into your first periods of actual trading, analyse the differences between your actual figures and the figures you forecast in your business plan.

The essentials of bookkeeping

Bookkeeping can be done inhouse or outsourced. Whatever option you take, ensure your figures are produced and analysed using a good accounting package or well-executed spreadsheets. Don't allow data to be left in the 'to do' drawer; clearing a backlog can cause errors. In computer science, the term garbage in, garbage out (GIGO) is where flawed or inaccurate data produces incorrect information or 'garbage'. Essentially, it means the quality of what you put in will determine the quality of what you get out. Do not allow this to happen – it goes without saying, but we will say it: you need accurate information to run your business.

Stock or inventory must be controlled either through a package purchased specifically for this purpose or on a spreadsheet. The choice depends on the volume and complexity of sales being achieved. There are many inexpensive accounting software packages on the market; Sage One is one of the more popular packages available and can be leased monthly for a small amount. If you use a package of this type, get to understand the accounts software so you become familiar with what's going on in your business. The profit and loss account should be analysed monthly and any variances to your plan will be highlighted with corrective action apparent. Set up reporting procedures so you receive information on a regular basis. Sales and your cash position should be monitored daily as any decrease in either of these, for whatever reason, will have a significant effect on the business.

Importance of stock turn

Stock turn, or the speed at which the stock is being replaced in the business, is a measure of extreme importance. You may have heard the expression 'just in time' manufacturing or production (JIT). It's used to explain a manufacturing or retailing operational methodology illustrating how a particular enterprise functions by only accepting the stock or product it actually needs on the day it needs it. For example, it might be the front end of a Mini arriving in the factory just as the car rolls off the production line to be driven away, or a box of Easter cards delivered four weeks prior to Easter and not shipped in before Christmas. The JIT car example is extreme and highly sophisticated, but consider this: if you trade with only the stock you need, how much higher your cash on hand will be compared to having a stock room full of merchandise you may not require for weeks. Stock turn or stock replacement is an area you must master.

Stock Turn

The basic calculation is:
   Cost of goods sold (A) ÷ Stockholding (B) = Stock turn (C)

To find the stockholding required for your business the calculation is:
   Cost of goods sold (a) + Stock turn (C) = Stockholding (b)

The outcome of your stock turn calculations will inform you whether or not you have the correct volume for bestsellers and will indicate the stock lines you need to consider re-ordering. Stock turns are normally calculated on the cost value rather than the sales value, as retail sale prices can be reduced during sale periods or if you have slow-moving stock. In contrast, the cost price remains static. To obtain the stock turn ratio, divide the cost of sales by the average stock. It should be noted that every industry works on different ideal stock turn ratios. We will discuss in more detail the difference between 'evergreen' and 'seasonal' retailers in Chapter 13 and clearly explain ideal ratios for a particular type of business.

You should analyse your stock weekly to spot slow-moving items. This slow-moving stock should be discounted as soon as you establish that there is a problem that cannot be resolved by other means. Your systems should also monitor your bestsellers to enable you to reorder to maximize sales. You want to keep your customers engaged by showcasing new product lines, too, and introducing new stock will keep your customers interested and encourage them to visit you more frequently.

The stock turn calculations example (see Figure 12.1) sets out different stockholdings based on annual sales of £500,000. It is evident that, as the stock turn increases, the stockholding reduces. A high stock turn of 6 requires only a stockholding of £25,000, whereas a low stock turn of 2 requires a stockholding of £75,000. This is a considerable increase, which will result in excess stock. Sales can also be affected by stock turn ratios. If your stockholding remains static and your stock turn ratio decreases, your sales will also decrease.

As a business grows, every successful retailer – no matter how strong the concept or how desirable the products it expects to sell – needs sound cost controls and accurate planning on how to spend resources. These are critical factors to get right. Too much capital or debt tied up in stock that takes too long to sell or that never completely sells out, without severe discounting, is a route to disaster. Ensuring the right products are in stock, in the right quantities, is crucial. This puts the emphasis firmly on merchandise planning and stock control systems, maintaining up-to-date stock commitment reports, and therefore the need to select an appropriate solution for your business. These are important decisions to get right at the outset and will generate confidence, improve budget control and set the right expectations for your business and your stakeholders. It will also declare your professionalism to those you may wish to raise money from in the years ahead. Planning expenditure in this way with an optimal target stock figure will both simplify and increase the accuracy of buying, purchase ordering and replenishments. A good system should continually calculate the best possible stock position for your business and ensure appropriate stock allocations before unnecessary replenishments. For fashion and clothing products, it will mean better precision in how you adjust size curves (also known as a

Figure 12.1 Example of stock turn calculations

A	Sales excluding VAT	£500,000	£500,000	£500,000	£500,000	£500,000
	Cost of goods sold	£150,000	£150,000	£150,000	£150,000	£150,000
	Gross margin	£350,000	£350,000	£350,000	£350,000	£350,000
B	Stockholding	£75,000	£50,000	£37,500	£30,000	£25,000	£21,429
C	Stock turn	2	3	4	5	6	7
	(Cost of goods sold divided by stockholding)						

size scale or ratio). Some retailers purchase too many small sizes and not enough large ones; Uniqlo made this mistake when they first arrived in the UK. It means there is less room for errors or impulsive outlay. You can maximize profits with the right amount of stock, in the right place, at the right time – all based on sound data.

In summary, be clear in your own mind what key areas of your business should be regularly monitored and ensure you are using the systems you choose to their full capacity. Having made the sensible decision to monitor your business carefully and thoroughly, think carefully about how you digest and react to that information. The greatest people in business and the most successful entrepreneurs always have people alongside them whom they trust and are prepared to share their concerns and ambitions with. Having a trusted person alongside you, who you can call upon from time to time, will help you enormously to make decisions. They can help you to move the business forward by questioning you, in a constructive way, on whether you are drawing the right conclusions from the data you have accumulated.

References and useful resources

https://uk.sageone.com/

Part Four
Buying and Visual Merchandising

Step one to procurement and merchandising

13

Understand your business and the marketplace you will be entering

Key points

Decide what type of retailer you want to be and understand that business

Buy to make money and manage stock appropriately

Control and measure product performance and KPIs

Build and maintain relationships

Customer behaviour and information overload

Customer feedback and the visual experience

Space performance and layout

Your global signpost

Choose whether to be an 'evergreen' or a 'seasonal' retailer

The evergreen retailer

An evergreen retailer sells a predictable and fast-moving selection of merchandise throughout the year. The stock held can be replaced on a next-day basis and is therefore not subject to the challenges involved in having to commit to the early buying decisions that are required of a seasonal retailer. Customers know what they are going to find if you are an evergreen business so they always expect to see the shop well-stocked with similar ranges throughout the year. Stock absorbs cash and the faster the evergreen retailer 'turns over' or replaces its stock, the more profitable the business will be and the more cash it will have to re-purchase stock – and pay the bills. An evergreen retailer should aim to completely replace, or turn over, its stock about twelve times per year. That equates to every four or five weeks. Some parts of the stock will turn over even faster. An evergreen retailer need never be overstocked.

The margin or gross profit (the amount of money between the price a business pays for a product and the price it sells it for) a business can earn in easy-to-replace merchandise is sometimes lower than in higher risk products such as fashion, cyclical or seasonal merchandise. However, the risk is lower. Because that risk is lower, it is unnecessary to commit and buy long periods in advance. An evergreen retailer holds no more stock than is absolutely required to fulfil anticipated demand. It will be the supplier to the evergreen retailer who will be holding the merchandise needed for replenishment. The supplier or manufacturer will be bearing that cash strain. It must be taken on board, however, that trading like this requires good, up-to-the-minute control, day-to-day knowledge of what is selling and forensic product analysis to take advantage of this process. The book addresses this vital point in Section Three on Finance and Control.

The seasonal retailer

A seasonal retailer, on the other hand, preparing to take a higher risk in exchange for a higher margin, must accept and understand the gamble of trends and therefore must be prepared to analyse and re-search the chosen market very carefully indeed.

A successful seasonal retailer will aim to renew, turn over or re-place its stock at least four times per year, which is every 12 to 13 weeks.

The retail year will be divided into two key periods: the spring/summer season that runs from February to July and the autumn/winter season from September to December. This timetable is not only controlled by the brands, but by the long-ingrained shopping habits of the consumer. The consumer, regardless of the prevailing weather conditions, will radically cut back on buying full-price spring/summer merchandise in mid- to late June and autumn/winter products in late November. The principal reason is conditioning to the seasonal sale periods, determined by national retailers.

A seasonal retailer should mark the weeks from late June to mid-August and late December to the end of January for sales or mark-down periods, 8 to 10 weeks of the year. It is, of course, preferable to enter the sale periods with too little stock rather than too much.

If 70–80 per cent of a season's purchases have been sold prior to the sale, then the business will have done very well indeed. Selling a lower percentage than this should trigger questions as to whether the collection of the particular product is in a 'high risk' category and should be dropped. Seasonal retailers must be radical retailers.

There is always surplus stock in the market if a business finds itself under-stocked and very often this stock can be purchased at lower than the original prices. The business can therefore achieve reasonable margins even at sale time. Remember, a good and open relationship with your supplier will often result in you being of-fered surplus seasonal merchandise at heavily reduced prices. Suppliers will always have overstock, often caused by cancelled or-ders or bad debts, but be careful you don't overbuy 'bargain' stock just because it's cheap. Another crucial benefit of not being over-stocked is that the business will be able to introduce new season stock early, in late July for autumn and in mid-January for spring. This will enable the business to stay one step ahead of the competi-tion, gaining the loyalty of the regular clientele and attracting new customers.

Seasonal retailer considerations

- Luxury/prestige: where customers pay exclusive prices for superior quality that delivers an aspirational sense of wellbeing.
- Brand: where customers pay for quality and brand name reassurance.
- Bespoke: where customers pay a premium to own a design or product unique to their needs.
- Value for money or affordable: where customers aspire to a 'lifestyle', but cannot afford a luxury brand price point.

Retail categories: evergreen

- Candles and incense
- Greeting cards and stationery
- Books, magazines and newspapers
- Crafts and related gifts
- Decorations (seasonal)
- Partyware and balloons
- Floral and related products
- Interiors and home décor essentials
- Home bedding
- Designer gifts
- General gifts
- Cosmetics, toiletries and wellbeing
- Housewares, hardware, china, glass, tableware and kitchenware
- Toys and games
- Delicatessen specialist
- Coffee, snack & take-away
- Baby clothing and baby gifts up to 3 years
- Specialty foods, grocer, butcher etc (can include seasonal foods)
- Cycles, cycle clothing and accessories
- Angling

Retail categories: seasonal

- Children's clothing from 3–12 years
- Adult/youth clothing from 13 years up
- Athleisure sports goods and clothing
- Shoes and accessories for men, women and children
- Fashion accessories, jewellery and fashion watches
- Furniture, lighting and soft furnishings
- Garden and outdoor products
- Leather goods, handbags and related gifts

Whether your business objective is to become an evergreen or seasonal retailer, the key points essential in building and establishing a brand are the same. You should always strive to:

- be different;
- be relevant;
- be constantly curious;
- be understood (the customers must grasp what you do instantly);
- build a reputation.

We remember hearing Angela Ahrendts DBE, Senior Vice President of Retail at Apple Inc and formerly CEO of Burberry, say strongly in an interview that customers today do not want to be oversold to. She also expressed in this interview that the role of today's retailer is to be an ambassador of the brand and to never lose focus on all the aspects that the customer will come in contact with. This will include window displays, merchandise displays, website, social media and, of course, human interaction. We agree with Angela Ahrendts and a perfect example of this view is manifested in the new Nike store on New York's famous Fifth Avenue.

From the moment the customer steps in to this Nike store, they are invited to experience what lies behind the famous brand. Customers are encouraged to interact with hi-tech video displays that explain how the products, particularly footwear, are assembled, designed, wind resistance-tested and engineered. Experts are on hand to recommend the right footwear for specific needs. Customers can design their own shoes using hundreds of options from laces to soles. These bespoke shoes will be ready in just two days. Kids can enter a special paint room to spray their unique footwear. All this gives a strong sense of how brilliantly the product has been executed by people who recognize the demands and needs of today's customers to have confidence in the purchase. Like Angela Ahrendts, Nike has not rested on its reputation but has energetically searched for ways to give the experience today's customers require, even subliminally.

Reputation matters. And your reputation is defined by the opinion that people you sell to, work with and trade with have of you and your company. It's about respect and admiration for the service they receive and the behaviour and character of the organization. Reputation matters more than ever in the world of retail and the main reason for focusing on building an excellent reputation is that it will help you to increase growth, make it easier to attract customers, and retain the best people to work and trade with you. Reputation creates trust and companies with excellent reputations have a far better chance of succeeding than companies with a poor reputation. It's a very valuable yet intangible business asset, earned by honesty, integrity, value, delivering consistent quality, service and authority of product, as well as the effectiveness of a website and bricks and mortar standards. Once a reputation is lost it is almost impossible to recover.

New brands grow through differentiation and relevance, and they achieve traction when they score high on being respected and understood. Established or well-known brands begin to die when they cease to score highly on differentiation and relevance, and instead rely only on respect and an old, misplaced understanding. They have entered the comfort zone – a very dangerous place to be for a retailer.

References and useful resources

D'Onfro, J (10 June 2014) '13 Angela Ahrendts quotes that prove why she's the perfect person to run Apple's retail business', *Business Insider* [online]. Available at: https://www.businessinsider.com/best-angela-ahrendts-quotes-apple-svp-retail-2014-6?IR=T

Efficient buying techniques to make money   14

Key points

Analyse your place in the market

Give your business brand authority

Plan your buying carefully

Stock turn

Develop your 'own brand'

Add value to your brand

Create a buying calendar

A retail start-up's place in the market

Whether the business intends to be an evergreen or seasonal retailer, it must be aware of the retail segment it is competing in.

As a start-up, be very aware of the financial size of the retail market in which you intend to operate. In the UK, very detailed information can be found on the Office of National Statistics (ONS) website, where retail statistical bulletins are published on a monthly basis. Bulletins like this, which are available in most countries, will clearly illustrate how the various segments in the retail market have moved over five- and ten-year periods.

When analysing these bulletins, focus on value rather than volume statistics, where value represents the money taken and volume the units sold. Value is a far better indicator on how a segment is performing. Additionally, in the UK, the ONS statistics are divided between large retailers, those who employ over 250 people, and small businesses, who employ up to 50 people. It is possible, therefore, to identify whether or not over the last five years the larger retailers have taken trade from smaller enterprises in specific segments. This may well help the decision-making process.

In addition to these statistical bulletins, website The Paypers provides very important information on cross-border online shopping. A recent article written by Robert Miller, featured in *The Times* of London on 12 September 2018, reported that the United States is the largest export market for British online businesses. United States consumers spent £12.5 billion on goods in the 12 months between August 2017 and August 2018. Chinese consumers spent £5.7 billion in the same period. Clearly, what you can take from this is that opening an online shop is truly an international enterprise. The Paypers site also allows you to drill into the e-commerce facts and figures in 25 countries, and analyses in some detail the preferred payment methods, online fraud prevention, e-commerce law and much more in each territory.

If you intend to establish a business in a local high street, it will be important to check whether a new shopping centre or superstore has opened nearby and has upset the balance of the area's trade – and possibly 'stolen' business from the local area. Even if that has happened, you can still survive, prosper and set your brand apart if you become an authority in the niche products you sell, provide high-quality service and employ relevant marketing techniques that appeal to your customer base. The right atmosphere in your store coupled with your online presence will be vitally important ingredients in providing a seamless experience that will leave your customers with an agreeable feeling towards your business.

A wonderful and successful example of this is an independent footwear store and online retailer called The Brogue Trader. Chris Macnamara founded the chain just over four years ago in Cardiff, Wales. His plan was to open ten shops in five years and he has just exceeded this by opening his eleventh store in Manchester. The Brogue Trader sells well-known British shoe brands and complementary products for men. The business prides itself on creating an atmosphere akin to a comfortable private members' club, complete with sofas and oak cabinets. The team are all featured on the website, wearing waistcoats, braces and bow ties, and offer one-to-one personal service.

Brand authority: what this means and how it is represented

A retail start-up's brand is key. Your new brand must recognize that consumers now expect retailers, both online and in shops, to offer an experience – as is demonstrated in The Brogue Trader example mentioned above.

What we mean by experience is customers' sensation upon entering the store (physical or online), built upon the following components:

- a quick understanding or grasp of the proposition;
- an impression of product specialism and know-how;
- ability to relate to your customers' aspirations;
- knowledgeable people (real and virtual) happy to serve and advise;
- brilliant use of space no matter the size.

A good experience will convey:

- Authority: What you do and know well, your skills and your specialisms coming through in everything you do.
- Personality: How you express yourself, how you 'look', how you 'feel', how you 'sound' and the total experience your business creates in every sphere of operations.
- Values: What you stand for, your beliefs, your personal and online service.
- People: Your staff, whom you need to ensure fully understand, and buy into, your brand, so that they can sell and talk about your business with both conviction and authority. This is the point of difference you strive for and which will set you apart from your competitors.

Be best in class

A start-up business has to be identified by its customer as being 'best in class' in the specific arena chosen – not just in a local area, and not just in the UK, but worldwide.

Social media and online platforms allow you to see what's going on in your market and, of course, permits your customers to remain hyper-informed. A start-up has to realize that today's well-travelled and well-informed customer has seen and experienced much, so the experience you offer really has to hit the mark.

Planning what to buy

Unique product selection

Very carefully selected and constantly updated products will ensure you stand out from the multitude of retailers on the high street and online. In recent years, the consumer has been overwhelmed by the volume of options, but has been underwhelmed when it comes to choosing a business that provides differentiation.

A new-to-market start-up has to realize that the hard work of a carefully selected and constantly updated product is their job. They are saving the customers search time whilst underpinning the value of the new brand and delivering the joy of discovery. So, choose special-ist products that provide your customers with an irresistible offering that they can find only with you. Always be aware of the competition, but don't copy them – be strong enough to follow your own vision.

Edit your offer

It is essential that you analyse your sales data and constantly ques-tion what to buy and what to stop buying. A new start-up does not need to buy expensive EPOS systems in order to do this; a simple Excel spreadsheet recording sales and ranking them by departments and categories will do the job. An example is provided in the next chapter (Figure 15.1).

You should ensure the planned purchases against the specific segments of your stock closely match your sales in those segments. For example, if 20 per cent of your sales are coming from greeting cards, 20 per cent of your stock should be in greeting cards, and of course 20 per cent of your spend should also be in that segment. It's seems obvious, but can be easily overlooked.

Most importantly, never guess what is selling well. Be ruthless: if a product is selling slowly against other products in the range, stop buying it and make sure you don't reorder. Always use your cash wisely and intelligently and remember that customers with fewer options are more likely to buy and will trust your edit.

Planning the buy

Once the selection of your product offer (merchandise) has been made and carefully financially evaluated, calculate the final cost value of what you are ordering before you finally commit. You should never buy more than you can afford.

The next stage is to ensure that the various products have the space to be displayed with authority and given appropriate position, while not overwhelming the shop or website. When you have this planned and ready to be executed, you should also have ensured your suppliers' products arrive with you at the right time to meet your customers' needs and expectations. For example, there is no point in Mother's Day cards arriving two days before Mothering Sunday or having heavy outerwear delivered in late November.

Essential planning checklist: key points to concentrate on

✓ To stand out, have a clearly defined buying and sourcing plan.

✓ Plan and financially evaluate, by segment.

✓ Ensure you are only stocking products in line with the overall business objective.

✓ Ensure the planned purchases against the specific segments of your stock closely match your sales in those segments.

✓ If you specialize in a segment, constantly scour the market for unique products to strengthen and refresh that proposition.

✓ Travel to trade shows if you can. International show guides, covering every possible type of merchandise, are easy to find on Google.

✓ Be cautious about importing from overseas if there is no agent or representative in the country you operate in, especially if you are asked to pay 100 per cent in advance or sign a letter of credit. If you can't obtain some form of insurance, it's best not to commit. Too many small companies have failed when overseas goods they have paid for fail to arrive.

✓ If you do import direct, cap the amount you spend. Overseas orders can be harder to replace so don't rely too heavily on one order.

✓ Occupy a marketplace that sidesteps having to compete primarily on price. Price wars are fatal and this is the case in online retail as well as high street retailing.

✓ Always keep some money back to refresh and update your stock. Ensure your choice is always consistent with your stated market position.

✓ Editing and analysing your sales (by every segment) is crucial. Carrying out this function monthly is ideal. It is important to carry out this vital task, using all the data from the stock and sales analysis, in order to 'signpost ahead' alerts that may need to be acted on.

Why stock turn is so important

As explained in Chapter 12, stock turn is a measure of the number of times stock is replaced over a period of time, for example over the course of a year, three months or even one month. How many times stock turn is measured is up to the business, but the more times the better. It's a fundamental measure because it represents how efficiently a business is deploying its cash. The equation to use for measuring stock turn is as follows:

Calculate retail sales, at cost price or at retail price, over the chosen period. Then divide by the retail stock held at the end of the chosen term, again at either retail or cost.

Note: it is important that you use either cost or retail price for both measures.

Example

Example 1: If sales amount (over the chosen period) is £1,000 and stock held (at the end of that period) is £500, then the stock turn equates to 2 times.

Example 2: If sales amount (over the chosen period) is £12,500 and stock held (at the end of that period) is £2,200, then the stock turn equates to 5.7 times.

Tip

Keep in mind your business will require a minimum amount of stock (by segment) to look authoritative and to achieve your sales plan in the physical space or screen space you intend to devote to it.

You should calculate stock turn in every segment to ensure you are not overstocked. For example, if sales of soft toys were £100 in the previous month and the stock held amounts to £75 (stock turn of 1.3), you are overstocked. This is an early warning signal; once you know this, you can consider and react. Maybe the choice was wrong or maybe the product is not being displayed correctly. Whatever it turns out to be, stock turn analysis will help to bring these issues to your attention. Normally, a stock turn score of 5 and above indicates an efficient business. An 'evergreen' business must turn stock faster than a 'seasonal' business because stock is always available from the supplier on short notice. Always check that the stock you sell can be purchased by return or on very short lead times, because any stock purchased in this way will benefit your stock turn. And increasing stock turn means money in your bank account.

Using cash wisely checklist

✓ Before you buy, always analyse your data.

✓ Develop a spreadsheet system of analysis, put dates in the diary and stick to them.

✓ Before you buy, carefully consider trends both inside and outside your business.

✓ Make sure everyone involved is participating by following a simple agenda.

✓ If you are working with colleagues, ensure someone is responsible for specific segments. This encourages responsibility and develops self-esteem.

✓ Always confirm and check orders (even telephone orders) before they are sent to a supplier.

✓ No matter how you communicate your orders, always keep hard copies, filed by supplier.

✓ When goods arrive, always match intake with your orders and check invoices. It's not unusual for suppliers to either substitute stock or add in more. In some cases, they under-deliver and that needs immediate follow-up.

✓ Don't accept late deliveries without carefully considering your options.

✓ Aim to hold back money to spend on re-ordering great sellers or to introduce product that you think will 'light up' your selection.

✓ Decide what percentage you can do this with and stick to it. It's common practice to hold back 10 per cent to 15 per cent of your annual anticipated spend for this purpose.

Developing a 'private label' or 'own brand'

A start-up enterprise can gradually develop a private label or own brand over time. Developing a private label or own-brand collection will underpin your business and your brand over the medium to long term.

Margin is the lifeblood of every business and products bearing a well-recognized brand or identity will always limit the margin you can earn. Retailing a product under your own brand will usually cost you less, but the price you retail it for will be close or similar to market levels thereby earning a greater margin for you. Don't rush it, but if the concept appeals stay with the objective. We will explain the steps to developing your own brand further on in this chapter, but first we summarize the importance of this below.

- A private label or own brand is a product that only carries your label or tag.

- A private label will set you apart.

- A private label will often give you a greater profit margin than merchandise from a recognized brand because the consumer will be unable to source the item elsewhere.

- Every business, regardless of size, needs to establish a private label.

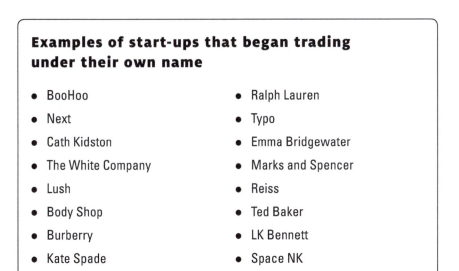

Examples of start-ups that began trading under their own name

- BooHoo
- Next
- Cath Kidston
- The White Company
- Lush
- Body Shop
- Burberry
- Kate Spade
- Ralph Lauren
- Typo
- Emma Bridgewater
- Marks and Spencer
- Reiss
- Ted Baker
- LK Bennett
- Space NK

Key steps to develop a brand identity for your own collection

1 Swing tags

Print a swing tag bearing your logo and brand to be attached to everything in the store and on every page on your site (even if initially the products sold are from various suppliers). There are hundreds of companies that produce tags at very low costs. For shop retailing, ensure the reverse side of the swing tag carries a removable price and product detail sticker. This can be used later for analysing sales.

By having your brand on everything you sell, you raise your brand profile and give uniformity to your proposition. You should also leave the tag on after you've sold the item – your customers will remember you and where they bought the item.

2 Analyse bestsellers by category

The important point when developing a PLC is to carefully analyse bestsellers in every category of merchandise sold. It is essential to trade for six months before taking a reliable reading of bestseller performance. Once the bestsellers in each category have been identified, you can then begin to source manufacturers of these types of product. (Visiting trade shows is the best way to do this.)

3 Determine items for your own brand

The size of your business will determine how many items you buy in each category to be selected for your own brand. You may even decide to begin with just one category; that's fine. The key point to always bear in mind is that when you introduce your product to the customer it must reflect the quality you wish to become known for and, of course, maintain. The item should include features and benefits that differ from, and are an improvement on, the closest branded product. Your customer will appreciate the exclusivity of your merchandise, especially if the selling price is similar to the branded product.

Adding value to your brand

Adding value to your brand or business is very rarely about price. Never confuse 'value' with low-prices and reduced-price retailers. The retailers whose marketing strategy wholly depends on delivering very low prices is becoming a very crowded area. The pound and dollar stores – Primark, PEP&CO, Peacocks, M&Co and Bonmarché in the UK as well as many others internationally – are fiercely competitive and it's an area that start-ups should avoid. The middle or value-added market is a far safer place to trade in.

Adding value is about the customer associating your business or brand with positive thoughts brought about by both their confidence in the product, the experience during the purchasing process and by offering consistent quality. The happiest customers shop in the independent sector, or in sectors where the 'iron grip' of the founding family still prevail. In order to succeed in this field, a retailer must be good – very good. Great brands become greater not necessarily by improving the product, but by associating themselves with aspirations such as events, celebrities and sports. We give some examples below.

Examples of brand associations

- Haig Scotch and David Beckham
- Rolex and Wimbledon
- Ralph Lauren and Wimbledon
- Hugo Boss with sports and the arts
- Emirates and world-renowned football clubs
- Chanel Perfume and Keira Knightley
- Louis Vuitton and art foundations
- Cartier and polo
- Uniqlo and Roger Federer
- IKEA with good food and an excellent crèche
- Starbucks and 'new' coffees

These brands have now created in customers' minds a link between their aspirations and the brand. Value has now flowed from the brand to the customer, who becomes an active marketer for that brand.

Clearly, a small business is unable to match the levels of association listed with these high-profile brands, but that is not to say you cannot begin the process of linking your brand to the lifestyle and outlook of your potential customers. For example, if a business sells to well-known people in its area, why not begin a celebrity board (with their permission) in the store and on the website and ask each celebrity visitor to write a few words about their experience. In most cases, people are more than happy to do this because it supports innovation and small business. Collaborating with local artists, hosting after-hours events and holding online competitions, alongside a regular flow of detailed product information and news blogs, all help to build the bridge and sustain connections.

Tangible examples of value-adds

- Include batteries with electronic toys, appliances or games
- Offer a hairbrush with a hairdryer
- Provide a garment cover and a clothes brush with clothes purchase
- Add a box of tea bags with a kettle
- Provide a recipe book with two pots of local produce
- Add a make-up bag with a cosmetic purchase
- Give a free stamp with two greeting cards

A brand will then gradually develop an identity through the relationship being fostered between the user and the product or service offered. The brand will begin to come to life in the mind of the customer and if the brand consistently delivers a 'top drawer' performance, it will endure. It can be hard work, but it's really worth it.

The buying calendar

Creating a buying calendar helps you to plan the buy and to put key events in the diary. It should include:

- trade shows, including trend analysis;
- planning for seasonal periods (Christmas, Easter, etc.);
- planning for sale periods;

- planning for special events;
- when your suppliers are due to launch their new collections or ranges;
- when you expect to receive deliveries.

The main function of this type of planning is to ensure that you source and place orders so that they arrive on time. The calendar will help you to look at the year as a whole and forecast the products that will be needed most at different times of the year. Your customers' needs and expectations change throughout the year, and they will expect you to anticipate their needs.

Your calendar also needs to take into account 'lead times' between placing your order with a supplier and their goods actually arriving at your place of business. If you have a physical store rather than just an online presence, you need to allow time for unpacking the goods, preparing them for sale and creating displays in addition to time to plan the layout for your website.

Be alert to your supplier's communications because they will trigger you to start thinking ahead to the different seasons and events that we have mentioned. More than a quarter of your annual sales will be in the last eight weeks of the calendar year so be prepared for 'Christmas in July'. It is in the height of summer that suppliers, retailers and the media are working on Christmas promotions, product choices and media plans.

As you work through your first year or two in the retail industry, you will be on a very steep learning curve – so be sure to make notes of the things that you have learned, both of the activities you've got right as well as the things you've got wrong. Then feed those experiences into your planning process, so in the coming years you become more and more efficient.

References and useful resources

References and further reading

Australia: http://www.abs.gov.au/ausstats/abs@.nsf/mf/8501.0
Canada: https://www150.statcan.gc.ca/n1/daily-quotidien/180720/
    dq180720b-eng.htm

France: https://www.focus-economics.com/country-indicator/france/
retail-sales

Germany: https://tradingeconomics.com/germany/retail-sales

United States: https://www.thebalance.com/u-s-retail-sales-statistics-
and-trends-3305717

Useful resources

https://www.ons.gov.uk/
https://www.thepaypers.com/cross-border-ecommerce/
https://www.thebroguetrader.com
https://10times.com/

Controlling and measuring product performance and establishing KPIs

15

Key points

Make data collection and analysis a priority

Use Key Performance Indicators (KPIs) to improve and monitor business

Analyse finances, merchandise and people productivity

Stock control: know what you're selling and capture every detail

Analysing a business's performance is crucial to controlling stock. Unless there are clear systems in place from the outset, it will not be able to achieve maximum sales. You need to analyse daily, weekly, monthly and yearly so there should never be any surprises. By constantly reviewing data and product performance, you will be able to react effectively to whatever changes are required. Remember, stock is money and needs to be looked after very carefully. Ensure you have a trusted stock control system in place and use it to track sales,

Figure 15.1   A simple spreadsheet example to keep track of business performance

This simple template can be analysed by sales performance, gross profit performance and product category performance and by supplier performance and product category performance, using the sort column. It can also be used as a commitment report.

A	B	C	D	E	F	G	H	I	J	K	L	M	N	O	P	Q	R	S	T	U	V	W	X	Y	Z	
sort column	W/C	supplier	product	prod categ	sku	size (if applic)	unit	cost	sales SPTI	vat	sales SPTE	margin %	gross profit	LW	%	LM	%	LY	%	LW	%	LM	%	LY	%	9
	21-Aug																									10
		3	toy	4	7001		1	£5.00	£12.99	20%	£10.83	54%	£5.83													11
		4	card	3	8001		1	£1.50	£4.99	20%	£4.16	64%	£2.66													12
		5	book	7	9001		1	£5.00	£8.99	0%	£8.99	33%	£3.99													13
		7	toy	4	7001		1	£6.00	£14.99	20%	£12.49	52%	£6.49													14
																										15
																										16
																										17
																										18
																										19
																										20
																										21
																										22
																										23
																										24
																										25
																										26
																										27
																										28
TOTAL							4	£17.50	£41.96		£36.47	50%	£18.97	£27.00	35.1%					£15.00	20.9%					29

margin formula: = (j11/1.2−i11)/(j11/1.2)

SPTI = sale price, tax included
SPTE = sale price, tax excluded

LW = last week's SPTE sales
LM = last month's SPTE sales
LY = last year's SPTE sales

measure stock turn and profitability and analyse performance by supplier and by product. (You'll recall we covered this in detail in Section 3.)

Be clear about what you need to benefit and improve your business. Too many businesses think they know what stock to buy simply because they are in the business every day, but this can be a dangerous mindset. Analysing the actual business performance is crucial to controlling both fast- and slow-moving stock in the various segments. In terms of value for money, a simple homegrown stock control system, demonstrated in Figure 15.1, is low cost and provides very rapid payback.

We want to highlight this point: unless sales are expected to exceed £1 million in year one, an expensive EPOS system is unnecessary. This simple spreadsheet will work extremely effectively for you.

Key Performance Indicators (KPIs)

KPIs or vital signs are early-warning indicators of how a business is trading. They provide historical facts and shape forward-planning. KPIs should be carefully selected and should include the contributions of everyone involved in setting up the business. Agreeing the vital signs and then monitoring them weekly will pay dividends. The people that have helped to agree them will also be invested in the decisions that arise from the business intelligence that are revealed, thereby helping the business to succeed.

The three KPI categories that really matter

1 Financial analysis

- Total sales
- Category sales
- Supplier sales
- Total gross profit*

- Category gross profit
- Money/overdraft

*See Section Three on Finance and Control of this book for how to calculate gross profit.

2 Merchandise analysis

- Total unit sales
- Category unit sales
- Category retail sales value as a percentage of the category retail value of stock. For example, if cards brought in 10 per cent of last week's sales, then the retail stock value held should be no more than 10 per cent. It's dangerous if cards brought in 10 per cent of sales and the stock held is 20 per cent. It means the business is overstocked in this category. If it's the other way round, the business is understocked.

3 People and productivity analysis

- Salary costs
- Average transaction value (ATV) of total sales. This is a very useful measure that will demonstrate if the business can grow its turnover by adding items to every transaction, which is a great way to build sales.
- Average transaction value (ATV) by employee. This indicator measures employee productivity and can be used for bonuses and targets.

You should measure all these three performances versus last week, last month, last year and against your plan.

Once you start getting measurable data back, prioritize the information and how it is used. For example, buy more or less or dispose of unwanted products. Put dates for a review of the data in the diary – daily, weekly, monthly, whatever is best for the smooth running of the business – and stick to it.

You should also be aware of the average transaction value (ATV) in each category of merchandise. For example, if the ATV in soft toys is £9.99, ensure your repeat buying reflects this. In other words, don't get overstocked with too many expensive soft toys above the ATV.

It may be that when starting out there is no formal business plan in place against which the KPIs in the business can be monitored; product may even have been purchased. This book emphasizes strongly the importance of putting in place, at an early stage, a business plan. If it is your intention to raise money (covered in Chapter 10), you will certainly be asked for a detailed plan, but a plan is still essential even if you intend to begin a business by funding it yourself.

TIP

Stock control and KPIs

Decide early on who will be responsible for inputting the spreadsheet data, who will receive the reports and who will review and act on the information.

Building and maintaining relationships in retail for long-term returns 16

Key points

Foster loyalty in your colleagues

Connect with your customers on several platforms

Maintain a good relationship with your landlord

Maintain good relations with your suppliers

Dual pricing

The team and your role

Start-ups can be a lonely business, but there will always be people you can trust and who can offer advice. Sensible and sometimes impartial contributions from a partner, a family member, a former colleague, an accountant, a lawyer, a relationship manager, a financial planner or a supplier are helpful and well-intentioned, but be careful.

Working with a sibling, for example, can create anxiety. If you do, it is essential to set up and agree on boundaries. The advantage, however, of working with siblings is trust. Operating in silos, where each person can do his or her thing, can be a sensible approach and can work well provided you have agreed regular meeting dates at the outset. For many siblings in business together, discussions never end. This is something you need to guard against – because time off is important, too.

Engaging colleagues, staff, associates as part of your business performance with a reward scheme will encourage success. If the team or those involved are listened to, and feel that their loyalty, commitment, passion and output are rewarded, they will be motivated and follow your lead enthusiastically. You need to be confident that everyone is doing their best to increase customer sales.

Include your team in the things you do for the business. For example, you can consider asking suppliers to deliver a briefing on their particular product to the whole team. It's likely they'll be more than happy to do so, and your team will be kept up to speed on products, trends and new ranges. As the legendary Sam Walton, founder of Walmart, said in his 1983 book *Sam Walton: Made in America – My Story*, 'The way owners treat their associates (staff) is exactly how the associates will then treat the customers. That's where the real profit in the retail business lies.'

Samuel Walton was an American businessman and entrepreneur best-known for founding Walmart, as well as Sam's Club. Originally Wal-Mart Stores Inc., it grew to be the world's largest retailer as well as the biggest private employer in the world. His book is excellent and one that we'd recommend you pick up a copy of. It's the story of a man's life, surrounded by a devoted and patient family and supportive friends, coming from the most humble of beginnings. It's also packed with useful tips that you'll pick up as you go on the journey with him, encountering his trials and tribulations as well as successes along the way. This book is not packed with formulae and retail cliché: it's about a man, his vision for retailing, and how he accomplished his dream by working with people, listening to them, listening to his customers and trusting himself and his family.

Customers and dual pricing

In order to buy effectively, you need to engage and connect with your customers. How can you do this? It's really simple: talk to them, either directly or through social media, and never rip them off with misleading pricing practices. Ask their opinion. Find out why they are buying or not buying, what they may want to buy in the future and what other needs they have. This will give you a valuable insight into what is important to them. We'll repeat it again: always listen to your customers.

You could consider inviting a core group of your customers to an event where they can give you feedback in a social setting, making them feel part of your growth and success. Other forms of collecting information and gathering feedback from your customers are through mailing lists, loyalty schemes, questionnaires following events, and social media reactions to your Twitter, Facebook and Instagram postings. The internet provides some fantastic avenues for understanding and engaging with your customers, so never stop using these communication channels. Work with the mantra 'earn their trust, keep their trust'.

One of the issues that infuriates us and misleads customers is the blatant use of dual pricing. That is, giving the impression that an item that has been marked down 50 per cent is a genuine bargain. The fact that the margin being made by the retailer at the reduced price is more than healthy illustrates a disregard for the customer through the misleading impression being given, and also demonstrates the ethos of the retailer.

The Chartered Trading Standards Institute (CTSI) is a professional association that represents trading standards for professionals working in local authorities, business and international consumer sectors and for central government in the UK. A long-awaited CTSI guide to pricing practices was released in early 2017 at the request of the UK Department of Business, Energy and Industrial Strategy and the Consumer Protection Partnership. The guide provides advice to businesses that sell products or services to consumers, both online and in shops, to enable them to formulate their pricing and promotional activity in a legally compliant way.

We strongly recommend that every start-up business should adopt and communicate to its clientele why a pricing practice or promotion is fair and not misleading – even if this is in a very small way. This is because, if challenged under the Consumer Protection from Unfair Trading Regulations (CPUT) 2008, that business will be required to show that it had a due diligence system in place to prevent misleading practices. This may sound onerous, but as long as you keep records of your promotional campaigns you will meet the due diligence requirements.

For example, when running a promotion involving a price comparison showing the business's original price and a discounted price, under the new guide you will need to be prepared to justify and document the answers to the following questions:

- How long and how recent was the product on sale at the higher price compared to the period for which the price comparison is made? Having an item on sale for a few days will invite problems unless you clearly mark it as a 'special purchase'. Please note, however, that a 'special purchase' can only show one price.

- Have you used a limited time or special terms around your offer? Falsely stating that the product will only be available for a limited time or that special terms for that product will only be available for a certain time, with a view to persuading you to make an immediate decision about the purchase, is problematic.

- Where products are only in demand for short periods each year, are you making price comparisons with out-of-season reference prices?

- Were significant sales made at the higher price prior to the price comparison being made or was there any reasonable expectation that consumers would purchase the product at the higher price?

What many will now find surprising is that, when answering those questions, practices that have been widely used by businesses for many years are now deemed under the guide as 'less likely to comply' or, in other words, more likely than not to be viewed as misleading and in breach of the CPUT Regulations. The guide offers practical assistance to those who plan marketing campaigns and pricing promotions, so we'd recommend sourcing a copy and keeping it on hand.

Landlords, concessions and suppliers

If you intend to have a physical presence, an open, honest and positive relationship with your landlord can only be mutually beneficial to all parties. Whether you have a lease or a short-term licence, it is vital to be on good terms with your landlord. Traditionally, shops have taken out leases on their premises. A lease is a contract that promises the landlord you will pay the rent for the duration of the lease period. However, things are changing worldwide since the 2008 recession. In the current climate, landlords are much more flexible about how they use their properties because they are obliged to pay business rates (in the UK) on properties that have been left unoccupied for more than three months. Landlords want you and they want the value of the property (on which they probably have a mortgage) to be maintained. In this climate, they are very likely to listen to your suggestions and be open-minded. If they know how you are trading – you can let them know by sending them your monthly sales – they are more likely to let you spread your rent if you are struggling. If you continue to struggle, and they remain aware, they may well keep their eyes open for another tenant and release you from the lease. The key issue is communication: you need the landlord and the landlord needs you.

Concessions

It is possible that your business may be invited to open a concession in a department store. It's proven a popular choice for online brands to take this route, so you should be aware of the terms of the concession agreement. Effectively, the department store is your 'landlord'. The store will take up to 30 per cent of your SPTE sales. The store will expect you to fit out the space at your expense and staff the space at your expense. So, unless your product can produce margins of at least 55 per cent to 70 per cent, concessions are not for you (see Figure 19.1). Normally, the concession agreement will allow the store to give a concession six months' notice (and vice versa) at the end of the initial term, normally two years.

Be very careful that the store does not try to shorten this period. If there is no such termination provision in the original agreement, then certainly do not allow the store to introduce one. Recently, a top London store attempted to remove a concession by claiming a termination period, but failed following a High Court judgment. This case demonstrated that making an application for an urgent 'interim injunctive relief' can help a brand defend its position.

Suppliers value honesty, loyalty, trust and being paid (in that order)

Suppliers are your source of product and therefore your source of profit and your business's prosperity. Building and developing relationships, whether direct source, agent or cash and carry is vital. Naturally, if you are a new start-up you may be asked to pay your suppliers upfront initially, but you will be treated very fairly once the second order goes in and trust develops. Suppliers don't like being dictated to by the very large retailers who can be demanding and disloyal. Many national retailers now routinely demand that suppliers contribute millions to new shop-fits, product placement and advertising support. Many have also lengthened payment terms.

Smaller manufacturing or distribution companies often can't manage this squeeze and therefore cherish relationships with small and medium-sized businesses. Therefore, they are often more accommodating and loyal; they like doing business with the independent sector. The relationship is important to both sides because having a large number of customers means suppliers can spread their risk. There are many good examples that illustrate this. Two good ones are TY (the makers of Beanie Babies soft toys) who refused to sell to the 'big boys' and consequently made a huge impact in the UK and the world with their independent-only strategy, and Ted Baker, who built the brand with independents that are still looked after by the company to this day.

Wholesale distributors and many product manufacturers work on narrow margins so cash flow is important to their business. A retailer, even a small one, that pays on time becomes a trusted customer. Some wholesalers track payment history in their customer relationship management software and even rate retailers based on how promptly they pay. Merchants with a good payment history may earn better prices or, eventually, get better terms. Since suppliers do have many customers and a number of relationships to maintain, it can also be helpful to learn what they need from you. Some suppliers will need specific documentation. For example, ensuring that suppliers have the proper documents, delivered in the preferred channel, can speed up order processing and an order might be shipped sooner. Once you have a reputation for paying on time or paying when you promise to pay, providing orders in the proper format, and being friendly and open with the supplier's representatives, you can begin to expect that the supplier will give you what you need. When it comes to marketing your business, ask your suppliers to notify you when new product images are available. Ask their permission before you use them and explain clearly where you want to use them. This will be much more cost-effective than organizing your own photo shoot.

Questions to address as you develop a strong supplier relationship

- Have you clearly defined your buying and product plan? Your supplier will appreciate this as they prefer their products to sit alongside complementary products.

- Do you buy from agents or direct from source? If you buy from agents for convenience, try not to. If you buy direct from source, you will see a bigger selection and you will be able to establish a valuable relationship.

- Do you use cash and carry? If you do, limit your use to absolute essentials as your margin will be affected. You would do better to start building relationships and establishing credit records with suppliers directly as early as possible.

- Do you utilize the expertise of your suppliers in merchandising and store layout? Suppliers have very clear ideas on how best to display their product and you can make use of this expertise.

- How frequently do you communicate with your suppliers? Try to meet regularly (certainly with your top five suppliers) even if it's not always to place an order, but simply to discuss trends, ranges and product information.

- Do you analyse each supplier's financial performance with the supplier? Take time to do this regularly.

- Do you ever ask for support from your suppliers for in-store promotional events and special customer evenings? Again, take advantage of their expertise in areas like this.

- Have you ever asked for special buys from your suppliers? Once you have a good relationship you can do so, which can be very useful at sale time.

- Do you explain to a supplier why you intend to stop buying from them if that becomes necessary? You should, because you never know, you may need them again. Part on good terms so that the relationship can be re-established when necessary for you.

- Terms of payment are crucial. Try your best to negotiate good terms and deals to ensure healthy profit margins and, of course, stick to the terms. If you can't, tell them.

- Be cautious about making an initial outlay on large volumes of stock. Even if you have bought at a discounted price, if you are left with a stockroom full of products you can't sell you will have made a costly mistake.

- Find suppliers who can sell to you in exactly the quantities you need. Don't be forced to buy more than you can digest.

- Who else are your suppliers supplying? Establish how this might affect your own trade.

- Can you reorder stock that becomes popular? It is important to establish this so that your store can adequately keep up with demand to make the most of popular items.

- You need to ensure that your suppliers can deliver when they say they will. It is no good receiving Christmas stock after Christmas – if they don't uphold their commitment and supply goods when you ask for them, you will need to send them back!

CASE STUDY Sherry Roberts CEO and founder, The Longest Stay

An alumnus of the Kellogg-WHU Executive MBA Program, this American living in London has always had a flair for business. Sherry opened a travel agency in her dorm room at university, started her career in telecoms, and had travelled to over 50 countries by the time she was 30. But her passion was always based on creativity and interiors – no doubt since she was educated from an early age to appreciate art, furniture and fine clothes. Roberts travelled widely and after two years of research across Europe, studying furniture trends, visiting trade fairs and understanding the new ways hotels were being furnished, she realized that many people would like to be able to buy the furniture or artworks they temporarily lived with, there and then.

Roberts quickly discovered that finding these pieces online was hard, so it became obvious to her to build a website that grouped this genre of furniture, lighting and home accessories together, making it easier for these customers to buy. The challenge then, as money was tight, was to assemble a team around her. She initially opted to employ students who wanted to gain work experience to help achieve their degree, but she struggled for continuity as these internships lasted only a few months.

Roberts wanted to raise money to fund a small team of fulltime professionals, which was when she was introduced to Rowland Gee, one of the authors of this book. The business sparks really began to fly and he brought a fresh pair of eyes to confirm issues that Roberts already knew needed to be rectified. They included the importance of sourcing skills, better due diligence on where else products were being sold, and at what prices. Gee stressed the importance of Roberts' endorsement of every product found on the site. This endorsement makes clear that Roberts personally selected every item and is also where Roberts adds extra information on the piece, giving a styling tip and an interior design idea. We think The Longest Stay is in a sweet spot in the 'home' luxury market and this will help the business to grow internationally. Roberts has also built excellent relationships with international suppliers and visits trade fairs constantly to ensure she keeps up to date with trends. And The Longest Stay's online marketing is top drawer.

Some people get it, others don't. We believe Sherry Roberts gets it.

References and useful resources

References and further reading

Vickery K and Williams, A (2017) No more '28 day' rule: pricing and promotions under the spotlight, Osborne Clarke [online]. Available at: http://marketinglaw.osborneclarke.com/advertising-regulation/no-more-28-day-rule-pricing-and-promotions-under-the-spotlight/

Walton, S (1993) *Made in America: My story*, Bantam USA, New York

Website

https://www.thelongeststay.com

Useful resource

https://www.hants.gov.uk/business/tradingstandards/consumeradvice/goodsandservices/pricinglaw

Understanding customers' behaviour and information overload 17

The need to make the product focused, visually clear and correctly price-positioned

Key points

Understand your customers' instore behaviour

Recognize that your customer is sophisticated and astute

Keep your offer clear and thoughtfully priced

Research, research, research

Customer shopping behaviour

We know that the pathway the customer travels on, both instore and online, involves eight key fundamental steps:

- awareness;
- involvement;
- comparison;
- consideration;
- purchase;
- consumption;
- relationship-building;
- recommendation.

Three-quarters of consumers today discover products online and through reviews. A similar proportion are influenced by value, trust, quality and service. Furthermore, 74 per cent of millennials would switch to a different retailer if they had poor customer service and 64 per cent of all age groups remain loyal providing the brand offers good value for money. Over 50 per cent of all consumers say that trust in a brand is absolutely key. So, get all the components right, earn the trust and keep earning it.

As we know, the way consumers now use the internet and social media means that they are very well-informed. Comparison websites mean that customers can compare product features and choices and discuss their views of a product with others. A great deal of product detail is available to consumers these days. For example, some sites give information that may relate to a product's ethical or green credentials; this is an important consideration for many customers and can sometimes even be the deciding factor in whether to purchase or not. When you are sourcing your products, it is therefore essential that they can be held up to scrutiny – customers will not think twice about interrogating social media and reviewing good and bad experiences! If your business has social media presence (which ideally it should), review the comments made on it carefully and regularly. The customer is more empowered than ever before. This is an opportunity as well as a threat to you. You can learn and react from opinion that is freely given.

Another point to make about current shopping habits is that today's customer is prepared to mix value and luxury. For example, they might use a low-cost supermarket for the bulk of their weekly food shop, but pick up a weekend treat from a specialist delicatessen. Today's consumer will team up a T-shirt bought in an outlet village with a pair of designer jeans. Customers no longer have an enduring sense of loyalty. They are often short of time and increasingly make their purchases at their convenience online. They will combine all the current retail options available to them: shopping locally, out-of-town, at supermarkets, independents, boutiques, online, markets, department stores and charity shops. The transparent economic climate dictates that you must get your pricing model 100 per cent in line with customers' expectations. If you don't, customers will desert you and begin to look elsewhere. Customers are spending wisely and everyone has their own set of ideas about what 'value' means to them. Customers are basing their purchase decisions on what they believe the product or service is worth to them.

Customers are easily able to make comparisons so your brand message needs to be clear and simple. In order to make it memorable, and to quickly show in which sector of the market you are unique, you need to really focus on what you're selling so that you are easy to understand and remember. It's a mistake to try to be 'all things to all people'. Your sales will benefit from a narrowing down of your proposition. It needs to be simple, clear and irresistible. Faced with too much choice, the consumer retreats to whatever they're familiar with and what makes sense to them quickly and easily. The new generation of shops, department stores and online sites are now 'curated' rather than stocked.

Ironic as it may seem, many dyed-in-the-wool department stores are now taking on the look of old-fashioned museums, whereas today's great museums are not only becoming brilliant at showing and lighting their exhibits, but have become great retailers through their artfully designed, cleverly laid-out and attractively presented shops. Confidence is catching, authority is energizing and humility is endearing. Your customers will pick up these emotions subliminally and respond enthusiastically to your proposition. We have attempted to capture these points using the easy-to-remember acronym, ROCC.

ROCC

- **Respect** is not bombarding your customer with too much information. This applies to email 'nagging'.
- **Order** is the logical way you lay out the store and the website.
- **Calm** is a well-laid-out store, appropriate music and a website that is 'calm' to look at and shop from.
- **Clarity** is all about your customer quickly understanding your product proposition.

Never stop asking yourself, your team and your customers whether your product is better and more interestingly presented than the competition. You should know why your customers should prefer to shop only with you. Ask yourself if you are creating the ultimate experience that your customers just can't find anywhere else and if you are continually challenging yourself. If not, your customers certainly will. Maya Nussbaum, founder and Executive Director of Girls Write Now, reinforces this point by saying that 'A retailer is someone who recognizes the need and comes up with a vision to meet it. A sustainable business is about keeping quality high, meeting new needs and innovating.'

CASE STUDY   Ted Baker

Ray Kelvin CBE, founder and Chief Executive of Ted Baker, had a pretty good idea what he wanted to do in life when he started working, on Saturdays, in his uncle's menswear fashion shop in London. This was 1966 and music, fashion, beauty, food and home design rules were being challenged and broken everywhere, with London leading the worldwide charge. This massive change in both outlook and acceptance of new ideas made a huge impression on Kelvin.

After he left school, he worked for various organizations, mainly in the product design and marketing areas. He listened and learned and realized early on that developing a 'private label' brand meant more product security and an opportunity to create aspiration. In 1988, at the age of 33, he opened his first shop in Glasgow.

His approach, at that time, was unique. (There was no world wide web, the internet only went live in 1991 and transactional selling didn't really take off until the 21st century.) He set out to create his brand through both the retailing and wholesaling routes. His initial strategy was to supply only the innovative independent fashion trade. He realized that this sector were influencers that wanted and needed new collections. He referred to this group of businesses as trustees, in effect trustees of his brand.

What we can see from Kelvin's approach is a determination to develop his brand more widely by being seen in shops that stood for his own individual fashion outlook. He recognized and tracked his customers' behaviour, the price bands that were acceptable to them, and he focused on the businesses that sold to this group. It was a brilliant tactic since the 'trustees' spread the awareness of the Ted Baker brand across the UK. This approach is a clear example of how Kelvin carefully researched the market and would not allow his brand-building strategy to be diluted and compromised by those who did not share his outlook. The team around him at this time was small and intensely loyal. The loyalty came because Kelvin trusted them, listened to them and made them feel 100 per cent involved.

When Kelvin met author Rowland Gee, then CEO of UK-based Moss Bros Group, in the mid-1990s, Ted Baker developed a new direction: tailoring. Gee persuaded Kelvin to produce a man's suit. Up to that time, Ted Baker had been a casual brand, but Gee insisted that every great menswear brand needed a suit. In Kelvin's unique way, he created a brand called 'Endurance'. Endurance would not be an ordinary man's suit – it would incorporate the very latest in non-crease fabric technology, would include internal pockets exclusively for mobile phones (now taking off) and have hidden holes for earphone cables. This product retained the Ted Baker design ethos and took the suit market by storm – and still does. Very soon after this, Ted Baker launched womenswear that is now responsible for 60 per cent of Ted Baker's total sales. International licensing followed in areas including eyewear, fragrance, tech, hairdressing and footwear (recently brought inhouse) that further secured the brand's strength whilst underpinning and delivering the customers' expectation.

Kelvin's story is about constant reinvention, innovation and team effort. With the Ted Baker website supporting international growth and a relentless focus on product and design, the clever use of social media and listening to his customers and the team around him, the brand has become a true competitor to the world's best-known clothing and lifestyle brands. And it all began from being a Saturday boy.

Kelvin is an excellent example of focus, determination and sticking to principles and being open with people.

CASE STUDY   Vagabond

Recognizing that your customer is sophisticated and astute, and thus prioritizing the need to keep your offer clear and thoughtfully priced, are qualities that are very well-demonstrated by Vagabond, founded by Stephen Finch eight years ago.

His idea and mission was to open wine bars where customers could pour, try and then pay for their wine choices with a top-up card. Finch created an experience and a meeting place that a specific demographic loved. People can move around the bars and sample from a huge selection of well-priced wines, exchange ideas and thoughts, and generally have a good time. Finch has employed a knowledgeable team around him that advise and interact with customers. So successful has this innovative start-up been that, following a pitch, Imbiba, a specialist investor in the UK leisure and hospitality market, has invested £3 million to help fund Vagabond's expansion. Rather like Harry Gordon Selfridge, who opened his store to everyone at the turn of the 20th century, Finch wanted to remove the pomposity found with many wine tastings. His bars and winery allow everyone to sample and discover wines, with no pressure, and in an informative and relaxed way.

This is a simple idea, but really well-executed. Finch had to ensure he had access to the wines he wanted and then check he could sell them at a competitive price that would leave enough margin to allow him to rent a high-street site. Vagabond is a superb example of defining the market it targeted, and then delivering what that market wanted. Too many start-ups believe they can manoeuvre the end-user to what the start-up wants rather than deliver what the customer wants. Always think through the eyes and minds of the consumer. It is no surprise to us that Vagabond was able to attract the funds for further expansion. Finch never lost sight of attainable and achievable margin, fixed costs obligations and people costs. You can be sure that Imbiba examined these cost centres very carefully before investing, so take from this the importance of careful planning and anticipation of what areas you will be scrutinized on should you seek finance.

References and useful resources

Websites

https://www.girlswritenow.org/who-we-are/leadership/staff/
http://www.vagabondwines.co.uk/
https://imbiba.com/

Useful resources

https://www.statista.com/statistics/792736/customer-loyalty-drivers-great-
    britain/
https://blog.accessdevelopment.com/customer-loyalty-statistics-2017-
    edition

Maximizing customer feedback and the visual experience

> **Key points**
>
> Make sure your brand message is clear and understood
>
> Pay very close attention to your window displays and home page
>
> Keep the inside and outside of your shop in pristine condition

It's a crowded market

How does a retail business stand out in a crowded market and differentiate itself in an increasingly competitive market? In challenging and low inflationary times, a business needs to maximize and demonstrate its unique selling points through its product, the way that product is merchandised, how well it is displayed and the people who present and explain it. These key principles are as important online as they are in-store. A retail business today, regardless of size, has to communicate its product offering quickly and clearly, both externally and internally. This is easier said than done.

Customer patience and attention span has declined dramatically in recent years. Online analytics tools will clearly demonstrate this through the time spent on a site and on pages within that site. It's frightening to see how rapidly customer choices are made. Today's customer is used to receiving (and expects to receive) data and information, digitally and audibly, in seconds. The same expectations apply on the high street. Business owners simply have to be aware of this and look at themselves hard. If a business recognizes that the first impression of windows, threshold experience, first-entry experience, product offer and positioning are what makes up the mind of the customer to either enter, stay or not, then that business will survive.

Points to take on board

✓ Be sure your customers quickly understand and 'get' your offer.

✓ Your business should both visually and physically clearly communicate the product it sells.

✓ Put in place a system to test your customers' understanding and reaction to your proposition.

✓ Ensure your website works efficiently; it will indicate to consumers that the business is 'always open'.

CASE STUDY   Cotswold Trading Company

Award-winning destination gift store, Cotswold Trading, started in 1992 with a tiny shop in Broadway in Worcestershire. In the early years, the family-run business offered a select range of gifts and housewares from compact premises. Right from the outset, they carefully controlled their stock and took very meticulous note of good- and bad-selling products. The business grew in confidence as they realized the range of products they were selling was meeting the expectations of their customers. In 1998, the business was transformed by the addition of a vaulted extension at the rear of the property, providing plenty of warehouse space to support the business both instore and online. The merchandise took on a more contemporary edge with inspirational must-haves and quirky collections to transform a home and garden into a truly special place.

Branded collections including Garden Trading, Cath Kidston, Voyage Maison and independent boutique designers including Powder Design, Bronte by Moon and Dash & Albert are displayed in dedicated areas of their own. Cotswold Trading has never looked back. The store now offers a one-stop destination for both gift and household items, attracting locals and visitors from all over the world, and the website features hundreds of the company's best-selling gift lines. It has become a magnet for customers needing gift solutions for all occasions without ever having to leave home.

Understanding your customer

In order to best respond to customer demand and expectation, you need to regularly get to know what your customers think of your stock and your business. Capturing specific sales data is imperative and will result in your money being spent wisely with both knowledge and confidence. That the 'customer is king' is a cliché, but it remains true. The difference is that the competition is no longer the store down the road: it is the whole world of retail.

Carrying out mystery shopping and online surveys are inexpensive and can be so useful. Another of the most effective ways of gathering feedback from your customer is through loyalty schemes. Think about hosting wine evenings in a shop to launch a new season arrival of stock or a pre-sale preview. They work. Genuine customers are generous with their opinions and you should make it known that feedback is welcomed, whether they are a customer or not.

If you employ people or intend to, ensure you regularly involve them by sharing customer feedback. Hold a monthly after-hours meeting in order to discuss what your team has learned on the shop floor. Try to understand from them why people don't shop with you as well as why they do. Ask your staff what they think of the relevance of your proposition and how it could improve. Hold twice-yearly Strengths/Weaknesses/Opportunities/Threats (SWOT) sessions (we covered this in detail in Chapter 3). Everyone should take part in these to get a really broad sense of how the business is progressing. Then write down and circulate the key points you have learned from colleagues. Make a note in the diary to follow up suggestions and observations. This is not only valuable as a record, but it also motivates those taking part to keep listening and keep sharing information and thereby improving customer relations.

On the outside looking in and displaying your best side

Your shop window display and your website home page are your first selling mechanisms. This has often been said and remains true. How many times have you passed a restaurant and not gone in because perhaps the lighting was too bright, the floor looked grubby, the waiting staff looked bored, the interior appeared shabby and the menu was peeling off the window? You made a decision without tasting the food. In this situation, we should feel sorry for the chef because he or she may have put extraordinary effort into buying and preparing delicious food, but customers are being turned off the restaurant by their initial impressions.

The medium, or the first impression, became the message. Your customer will make a similar split-second decision about your business. First impressions will not deter the customer who already knows you well, but remember that your business is always looking to recruit new customers who have never visited your enterprise before.

Once you are satisfied that the product you buy fills a relevant niche in the market and one where you feel you can make money, and you are satisfied that your customers and team understand and support this proposition, you must turn your focus to the physical layout of your store and the shopping experience within it.

You don't have to look far to find world-class examples of outstanding internal layouts that showcase products in the best possible way. Some of the businesses we think that achieve this include Whole Foods, Uniqlo, Burberry, Anthropologie, Pottery Barn, The White Company, Zara, Chanel, Pret a Manger, Cotswold Trading, Louis Vuitton, Gail's

Artisan Bakery, Selfridges, museum shops and ShopDisney. These operations use their store layouts to provide both high-quality and value-shopping experiences and demonstrate clear propositions. The standards employed are carried through to their websites. Smaller businesses often don't enjoy the luxury of space and can be inclined to cram in merchandise that there is little room for in the physical space. This is actually a big turn-off for customers. The process of editing or curating your product offering and allowing 'breathing space' is crucial. Remember, the 21st century customer is widely travelled and has seen the best and dismissed the worst of internal layout and display. Even if you do not have the latest equipment to show off your product, you can guarantee that a tired and dusty shop or a website that displays 'sold out' stock will put off your customer. Always make your product spring to life with well-thought-through internal displays and piercing directional lighting. (Remember in particular that fluorescent lighting, albeit inexpensive to run, bleaches the product!) Even the very finest stores like Louis Vuitton constantly review and challenge their layouts and the latest format in Paris.

'The medium is the message' is a phrase coined by Marshall McLuhan, introduced in his most widely known book, *Understanding Media: The Extensions of Man* (1964). It means that the form of a medium embeds itself in the message, creating a symbiotic relationship by which the medium influences how the message is perceived. A symbiotic or interactive relationship brings together two parties, where each depends for its existence and profile on the other. For example, this relationship exists in a shoe repair booth that stocks shoe polish, shoe trees, laces and other complementary products. These products need each other. The phrase 'the medium is the message' was exemplified when world-famous photographer Annie Leibovitz brought together the original James Bond, Sir Sean Connery, and Louis Vuitton for an advertising campaign. Another great example of the medium underpinning the brand is UK cycle company Rapha, which has opened stores or 'clubhouses' across Europe, North America and Asia. In the clubhouses they organize escorted group road rides and social spins. They arrange panel discussions and workshops, or you can just enjoy the excellent clubhouse café. Paul Smith is designing a new collection of cycle clothing for Rapha and the latest Brompton bikes can be hired for a test ride.

Consider carefully the look and maintenance of your shop – its frontage, windows and entrance. Use the checklist below to ensure you are covering the essentials.

Covering the essentials of shop maintenance

- Aim for simplicity, clarity and style, whatever you sell and wherever you sell it.
- The proposition must be clear, less is more and always 'tell a story'.
- The merchandise must be attractively presented and always well-lit.
- Backdrops must be relevant to the display, clean and uncluttered.
- If displaying fashion, the accessorizing must be as thoughtful as the clothing choices.
- When displaying electrical products, the detail and precision of the product should be respected in the display. For an example of good practice, consider how John Lewis or Apple display small electrical items, china, toys, bags, etc, providing the customer with ample information.
- When displaying gifts, give every category its own dedicated space.
- Foods should always be displayed in specialized categories. For fantastic examples, take a look at Whole Foods.
- Clean the blind regularly if you have one as well as the fascia, the windows and front door every day.
- Ensure nothing is taped on the window or door unless it's a properly laminated sign or a decal (transfer).
- All signs (for example, opening hours) must be inside the glass and ensure your website address is at eye level.
- Check all external surfaces are painted and freshly cleaned.
- Check all fascia lights are working as well as your projecting sign (if it is electrical).
- Check the window ceiling is clean; remove all unused hooks.
- Check the window floor is clean: dead flies are a no-no!
- If used, mannequins should be clean: no chipped heads or taped arms!
- Mannequins should be correctly positioned.
- If used, metalwork, tables, surfaces or props should be clean.

- Price signs (if used) should be neatly displayed and correct! Hand-written signs fade so must be regularly replaced.

- Cast a critical eye over your window display every day and change it every two weeks, even if you replace the same product. It must look fresh.

- Ask a supplier, from time to time, to dress your window. They are usually keen to do this and may well do it free of charge.

- Ensure clean pavement outside and the door mat (no chewing gum marks).

- Ensure clean shop floor right up to the walls and vacuum the ceiling.

- Ensure clean fixtures, cash point, shelves and work surfaces, including all metalwork.

- Ensure clean and correctly direct all light fixtures inside the window and shop and ensure every lamp is working.

- Ensure only essential information is displayed by till and PDQ machine.

- Working, audible and appropriate music, if used.

- Well-thought-out wall area behind the pay point. No sellotaped messages, anywhere!

- Well-presented team.

- Clean fitting rooms and mirrors, if needed.

- Fitting room stools and wall hooks.

- All painted surfaces to be regularly maintained.

As we have strongly recommended, a business today, regardless of size, has to clearly present and communicate its product, externally, internally and online. There are many written and online examples on the subject of window display, visual merchandising and home page design that you may wish to explore. For inspiration on setting up and designing your displays, browse through Pinterest or Instagram.

CASE STUDY   Blue by Jan Park

Established over 16 years ago, Blue by Jan Park is a small department store based in a three-storey period building in the old market town of Shifnal in Shropshire. As the head of the business forum for Shifnal and the owner/manager of Blue, Jan

Park is a passionate, open-minded and forward-thinking retail professional. When she became aware a few years ago that mentor advice was available she decided to engage Grey4Gold, Rowland Gee's mentoring company.

After a successful career as a university lecturer in art and design, Park moved into retail a number of years ago, but her professionalism and passion for the business still burns just as brightly. Blue is already being used as an unofficial centre of retail excellence and you can see why. Park listens to her customers and they respond. Like many of the retailers in the town, Park is incredibly knowledgeable and passionate about what she does, but she is equally clear that Blue is a business and needs to be profitable. She is just as comfortable talking about margin and profitability as she is about the latest trends.

When we met Park in her beautiful store she said, 'People just don't recognize the breadth of skills and experience you need to run a successful retail business. It's a profession and you need to treat it as such if you want to succeed. Having an experienced retail mentor to support me, even just to reassure that I was getting it right, was invaluable.' Visiting Blue and hearing from Park how she approaches every aspect of her business, it was possible to see just why she is so successful.

We think Blue is certainly getting it right by creating an 'experience' – encouraging customers to spend time and not necessarily money in its premises. Ice cream corner, coffee shop, art gallery and regular exhibitions have all created a friendly destination for locals and visitors to the area. Park is always checking on the sales she gets in various categories to ensure every category pulls its weight. Blue works hard to source its products from as many British and Fairtrade certified or ethically sourced makers as possible. The store carries a number of well-known brands alongside many small, individual designers. The Thread is a ladies' boutique inside Blue, where many of the clothes are made in Britain and all of them are ethically produced and made from natural fabrics. This is another excellent example of McLuhan's famous phrase we introduced earlier in the chapter.

References and useful resources

References and further reading

Bianchi, J (6 Sept 2016) '6 Visual Merchandising Tricks to Increase Your Sales Per Square Foot', Shopify Blog. Available at: https://www.shopify.com/retail/6-visual-merchandising-tricks-to-boost-your-sales-per-square-foot

Earl, A-M (8 Aug 2017) 10 visual merchandising ideas you should steal, *Gifts & Decorative Accessories* [online]. Available here: http://www.giftsanddec.com/article/545402-10-visual-merchandising-ideas-you-should-steal/

McLuhan, M (1964) *Understanding Media: The extensions of man,* McGraw-Hill

Raducan, V (3 Dec 2018) 'Why These 25+ Website Homepage Designs Work So Well', Extend Themes [online]. Available at: https://extendthemes.com/homepage-design/

Websites

www.blue-shifnal.co.uk/
www.cotswoldtrading.com

Useful resource

https://www.pinterest.co.uk/melindabp/window-display-ideas/

Visual merchandising

19

Managing space performance,
layout and add-on selling to
encourage purchases

Key points

Calculate the space performance of your store

Use analysis to work out where to physically position your products

Understand add-on selling and feedback

Gather customer feedback to constantly improve your store

Measuring and analysing space performance and add-on selling

How to calculate space performance

Earlier in the book we discussed the importance of controlling and analysing the 'buy'. It is imperative to understand the importance of measuring the performance of the product in the space devoted to it instore and online. Using the sales data analysis set out in Chapter 15 (Figure 15.1), space performance is about giving sufficient space to merchandise that is selling well and to not allow poor selling product to occupy too much space. If 10 per cent of the space in a shop is allocated to cards, for example, then cash sales should match that.

Let's say a rectangular shop occupies approximately 90 square metres of floor space, measuring 6 metres wide by 15 metres deep. It will have a left and right wall and one back wall. The sidewalls will usually measure 2.5 metres high by 15 metres in length (this is termed linear space). The two walls will therefore total 75 square metres. The back wall is 6 metres wide by 2.5 metres tall, equalling 15 square metres. Altogether (combining the 90 square metres floor space plus 37.5 square metres side wall capacity and 15 square metres rear wall capacity) the shop has 180 square metres of 'displayable or useable' space.

No store uses all its space, of course. There are doors, pay points, display areas, changing rooms (if needed) and team space to take into consideration. Let's say this shop will therefore have 140 square metres of the 'displayable and useable' space remaining after these other requirements are deducted.

If the shop devotes a wall fixture to a display of aromatic candles that measures 3 metres long by 2.5 metres high, it will equal 7.5 square metres, or just over 5 per cent of the 140 square metres available. If the candles produce 5 per cent of annual sales, that's great. If, however, they produce 15 per cent of sales, buy more candles and give them more space; if they take less than 5 per cent of sales, reduce the space you allocate to this product.

Simply put, there ought to be a direct relationship between the amount of display or fixture space given over to a product and the quantity of sales achieved by that product in that space. Take time to study this relationship in your store using the data. It's a way to double-check the product performance and will help you refine and define what you sell and the space you have given it. This is space performance. It is used by the most sophisticated retailers to measure every level of performance and will also be used to judge the contribution of store concessions.

How to work out where to place your product

Having analysed the space performance of what you sell, you are now in a far better position to decide where the product should be positioned physically. This applies to product placement on a website too. Some retailers decide to place 'hot' selling products in secondary locations so other slower selling items can be viewed earlier. This approach is fine, providing that the popular product's performance does not suffer as a result. Customers like change and 'freshness', but do not like to feel confused. If, for example, they are used to seeing fashion accessories in a certain location and the display has been moved, then they might not go looking for it in its new location. What really matters, however, is the space performance analysis. Be sure to keep up your data work to check that a product's performance has not suffered by physically re-locating it. These analyses have to take preference over a subjective intuition – the figures are a direct reflection of what your customer is telling you through what they buy and what they leave on the shelf.

Understanding the value of add-on selling

Add-on selling, in a shop or online, is all about confidence in what you sell. Developing confidence is helped considerably not just from implementing stock and sales analysis, but also from the relaxed (after-hours) sessions you hold with people involved in the business. Involving the team is absolutely essential in any business regardless of size.

Add-on selling, also referred to as 'upselling', represents a source of significant extra sales, and profit, for every company or enterprise that adopts the approach. We have all bought items on Amazon and, before we have even checked out, complementary products have popped up as suggested add-ons to our purchase. Even small businesses can integrate many features into a transactional website, including suggested add-ons. It is possible, using a software program such as Magento, to set automated rules to determine which products to present as add-on selling options together to each customer's original selection. Rules are easily administered through a tool allowing you to choose product suggestions, thereby increasing sales and average transaction values. Very few alternative platforms give you the power to efficiently create your own shopping experience.

Figure 19.1 Concession model

Any corner		
Square metres allocated		46
Sales PSM including VAT		£7,535
Total sales including VAT		£350,000
Sales per week		£6,731
Annual sales net of VAT		£291,667
Gross profit	55.00%	£160,417
Cost value of stock		£131,250
Staff cost per hour including NIC	pay	£11.00
	hours	35
	weeks	52
Payroll cost	FTE	2.5	£20,020
Salary to sales (incl. VAT) ratio	4.77%	£50,050
Operating profit		£110,367
Notional concession rate	29%	£84,583
Profit after concession fee		£25,783
Weekly service charge (flagship)	£80	£4,160
Corner's profit after all costs		**£21,623**

HN investment

Shop fit costs PSM	£484	£22,500
Initial stock pack turn	3.5	£37,500
Total HN investment		**£60,000**
RETURN ON CAPITAL EMPLOYED		**36%**

Notes

Sales are PSM (multiply PSF by 10.764)

Sales for the purposes of this model are set at over £7,500 PSM (high against national averages)

Concession rate Row 17 should be calculated on Sales excl VAT

Shop fit costs calculated on PSM

Salary to sales (incl. VAT) ratio

Salary costs are very low – normally 12%–17% of sales excl. vat (hours are 40 per week and you have to allow for holiday cover)

Gross profit is set at 55%. This underpins the need to get nearer to 65% so as to allow for sales fluctuations.

Concessions are risky since high sales and margins are vital, privale label is the only option.

Other benefits available on this particular platform include the ability to quickly create a website designed for every type of device. The themes allow you to adjust how menus, images, checkout and other features look, ensuring that they are both user-friendly and easily customized to suit your business. You can also work on ways to drive higher sales by sorting products by bestsellers, by new styles, by colour, and so on.

When it comes to add-on selling in a physical shop, engaging in conversation is very important. Customers simply being acknowledged is more important than you think and is increasingly rare. Don't begin with 'Can I help you?', as it nearly always provokes a negative response. It's actually far better to just say good morning or good afternoon and then to go on to explain what new product has arrived. Naturally, if you do engage, knowing all about your stock and being able to talk knowledgeably about specific features or product benefits will impress your customer and won't come across as 'hard selling'. Try to treat each client in an open and honest way. Once a comfortable relationship has been established, you can begin to introduce products that complement their original choice or area of interest. That's service. Large store operators who don't employ the people to provide this kind of personal service think very carefully about positioning products that they believe can be added on to an original purchase. It's their attempt to add-on selling.

Gathering customer feedback

Feedback from your customers is a priceless source of information and far more useful than outside research. That can be expensive, as well as sometimes inaccurate and misleading. We list below several ways in which you can gather feedback from customers, which will both reward their loyalty and help you to gain insights.

Feedback routes

- Feedback on a live chat session.
- Feedback forms on your site or instore.
- Contact customers regularly with news flow.
- Email surveys for new customers.
- Use social channels.
- Feedback on order confirmation page.
- Use polls.
- Create an online community.
- Employ loyalty schemes.
- Display positive as well as negative customer feedback to show honesty.
- Personalize your online store.
- Feedback in return for a prize or gift or discount on a future purchase.
- Ask for feedback immediately after a purchase.

Collecting customer feedback is an important part of the business process. Obtaining positive as well as negative feedback is equally important. Fortunately, as we have indicated, there are many ways to generate feedback. Some of these methods will give you ideas how you can get quality customer feedback from both shop and website. Some companies ask for feedback, but don't do anything with it. Positive feedback is terrific and negative feedback can be really irritating, but you still need to face up to it. Look at the answers, put a date in the diary to scrutinize the lessons learned, establish headings, categorize responses, then carefully analyse the feedback so you can implement changes, if you believe these changes will improve the businesses performance. Analysis like this will reveal both good and bad patterns and will give you important leads to improve.

References and useful resources

Further reading

Ciotti, G (14 Feb 2018) 'The 8 Best Ways to Collect Customer Feedback', Help Scout [online]. Available at: https://www.helpscout.net/blog/customer-feedback/

Websites

https://magento.com/products/magento-commerce
https://www.optimonk.com/

Creating your global signpost through online merchandising

20

Key points

Know what type of retailer you are

Communicate the difference you bring to the market

Understand why being effective online is vital

An effective online presence

The retail industry is a wide-ranging sector with businesses of many different types involved. It is a dynamic and highly competitive industry, which needs to respond to customers' demands 24/7. Consumers expect to buy every type of product online or at least be aware of a business through an online site or through social media channels. Your website is your global signpost and your social media are vital selling routes. A retail operator's website has to be transactional – it can't simply be informational.

A fully functional transactional website is your online shop window. Your website should:

- market the shop;
- state the services the business offers;
- introduce the people who operate and run the business;
- promote instore events;
- display and refresh stock;
- suggest and introduce complementary add-ons;
- explain and promote loyalty schemes;
- have a professional checkout system.

The website should encourage customers to come into your store and could even feature a short video to give a virtual tour of the shop or to hear from its owner explaining the new stock. Always remember that running an effective and successful e-tail site is like having a shop, just as if it was on a high street with its own individual flavour. As we covered in detail in Chapter 8, when we discussed creating an on-brand website, a unique product offering and attractive branding will be what attracts customers to your online store rather than searching elsewhere. The way to achieve this and provide a high-quality shopping experience online will be down to how you decide to build and design your website. The look and feel of it is just as important as the look and feel of a physical shop. Customers need to understand immediately what you're selling. Above all, the website must be simple to use and functional.

Alastair Browne, Head of Site Research and Strategic Insights at JD Sports, said recently at the 2018 Drapers Online Forum, 'We have looked to embrace the whole omni-channel approach to retail, offering the consumer the opportunity they demand to shop with us anytime, anywhere.' He went on to say, 'The store remains a key channel of sales.' Notwithstanding that, he recognizes that providing the consumer with an exciting and relevant online experience is essential.

Once customers have bought from you the first time or have subscribed to your website to receive information, you will be able to use their email addresses (subject to data protection) to get in touch with them about offers, new products and special events for privilege customers. Your website will also provide a significant amount of information including how many new visitors you've had, how many repeat visits, the pages they are viewing and the percentage of those who convert into a sale. You'll also be able to find out where your online traffic comes from and where people are finding out about your business. This feedback from customers is invaluable information that can be fed into your planning.

Continually ask yourself the following questions about your website:

- Are you constantly refreshing and updating your product?
- Is your choice consistent with your stated market position?
- Are you focusing on the importance of deleting 'sell-outs' and near 'sell-outs' and maintaining good stock control online?
- Are you thinking about the next step to refresh and invigorate the site?
- If you operate a bricks-and-mortar store, do you 'cross market'?

Magento and Shopify are two eCommerce platforms that support and empower thousands of retailers and brands with transactional websites in order to rapidly innovate and grow. They are each worth having a look at as best practice examples. As further examples of best practice, the following two case studies will look in detail at one retail start up that created a transactional website with online merchandising that complements the overall business strategy, and another start up focused on perfecting its own website to showcase bespoke software.

CASE STUDY   The Baby Cot Shop

After spending time in the United States, interior designer Toks Aruoture started specializing in baby and child interior design and developing a range under her own brand. When she moved back to the UK in 2008, Aruoture decided to launch into the highly competitive UK retail market.

The company began as Punkin Patch Interiors. The first piece of advice she took from Rowland was to change the name of the company so that it could be more easily found online and the domain name would align better with the company's products: hence The Baby Cot Shop was born. Rowland advised her to focus initially on securing her manufacturing suppliers; to design and build a transactional site that clearly explained her journey, her product specialism and her ethos; to gradually begin a search for a concession opportunity; and then look for a shop of her own.

Department stores today are always searching for new brands to fill their floors with excitement. Aruoture was encouraged by Rowland to not just call them, but to produce a piece of computer-generated 'imagineering' so the store could easily understand how The Baby Cot Shop could look alongside other concessions on their shop floor. Aruoture landed a contract with House of Fraser, an eighty-store UK group, who initially placed her products on their online site. This was invaluable experience as she quickly discovered the power of online trading and the importance of product placement.

In the meantime, a shop opportunity in an affluent area of London near homes and schools came up in late 2016 and she grabbed it, but not before negotiating a good deal with the landlord. This shop would give her the space to show off room settings for the product and would give her terrific content for her Instagram marketing strategy. Instagram now brings shoppers into her shop and keeps the business growing.

What really impressed us was that she took our advice to both secure her manufacturing resources and to develop an open and friendly relationship with those factories. The principal factory she now works with is based in Romania. As Aruoture quickly recognized after investigating many countries and sources, Romania is the home of many seasoned artisans who use traditional methods of craftsmanship and who produce made-to-order, hand-decorated and hand-assembled furniture. So good has her relationship become that she recently told Rowland, 'The factory will produce five of every design I give them, but only invoice me when they ship one. They are happy to take the financial risk.' This illustrates clearly what we talk about in this book. Develop a relationship with a supplier, be open and honest and you will be pleasantly surprised what you may get in return. Aruoture keeps adding to her designs and continually shows on her Instagram posts how beautiful a child's bedroom or nursery can be. Toks Aruoture, mother and business owner, can be found in her shop four days a week.

CASE STUDY   Brand Lab Fashion

Dan O'Connell and Jennifer Drury, Chairman and Chief Executive Officer respectively, and co-founders of Brand Lab Fashion, are the definition of what can be achieved with a singular vision, steely grit, drive, resilience and a good sense of humour.

In 2018 the company was valued at over £20 million, had a database of over 10,000+ retailers and 200+ brands increasing at a rate of 15 brands a month. Brand Lab Fashion is quickly growing to be one of the most innovative fashion technology solutions at the forefront of the industry and a business to watch.

However, roll back three years and 2015 marked the start of a challenging, but ultimately rewarding journey to success. Following independent careers within finance and fashion, O'Connell and Drury shared a common vision for a global digital fashion business that would disrupt the traditional wholesale model. Witnessing at first hand the dwindling footfall and rigidness of business at trade shows, not to mention the financial burden for retailers travelling across the globe with their buying teams and the increasing cost for brands to build creative, immersive stands, Dan and Jen saw an opportunity to break the current mould and shift the wholesale 'trade show' industry to digital.

Armed with their game-changing concept, Dan and Jen initially visited local business people and investors, but received knockback after knockback from businesses who didn't share their vision or thought a digital fashion company based in south Wales wouldn't get off the ground. Undeterred, they received interest from a software academy owned by a famous Welsh billionaire who believed in their product and offered to back the business and build the platform as a partnership. However, during the late stages of negotiation, the billionaire's colleagues who were leading the negotiations demanded 90 per cent of the profit along with ownership of the IP, leaving Dan and Jen with all the risk and no control over the business's future.

Walking away from a deal, albeit a one-sided one, was a huge disappointment and one that was met with negativity and disparaging comments telling them that they would never make it work, never build the product and never get to market. Frustrated and upset, but with even more determination to succeed, it took three months to redevelop a business plan and get the ball rolling whilst simultaneously running their exiting joint venture, fashion agency Red Storm.

Throwing caution to the wind, Dan and Jen contacted several investors via cold calling-style messages on LinkedIn. Out of 50 contacts, they received the one reply they needed. Unbeknown to Dan and Jen at the time, they'd caught the attention of a fashion investor whose family own one of the biggest retail conglomerates in Ireland. The tycoon invited them to meet in London and discuss the venture. Selling their laptop to cover the train fare to London, the future of the business was in Dan and Jen themselves; the prospective investor would need to buy into their passion and belief in their business concept. Having successfully secured the investment they required to take the business to the next stage, a series of further investment drives quickly followed. This enabled the team to focus on the website build and software development.

Proud to be an innovative Welsh business, Dan and Jen were keen to maintain the head office in Newport and established a highly skilled team of UK marketing and creative professionals to drive the business forward. The site launched mid-2017 and, despite not having a marketing budget, thousands of retailers signed up in the first six months, including prestigious brand wins such as luxury French label Paul KA and global fashion brand AX Paris.

Fast forward to 2018, the flourishing business secured an exclusive financial partnership with the UK's fastest growing online lender iwoca, providing an unrivalled service for retailers. The head office team has continued to grow and provide excellent employment opportunities within south Wales.

The future of Brand Lab Fashion looks bright with a move to larger headquarters in south Wales and the business set for global expansion with presence across Europe, Los Angeles and New York throughout 2019. The whole story is one of determination, belief and the ability to carry on after getting knocked down again and again.

It also goes to prove the old adage that if you haven't got passion, you haven't got anything. Never deterred, this company has shown tenacity and confidence in their ability. They focused on their website and created a bespoke technology function that resulted in a unique, fully integrated fashion wholesale platform that we think will set Brand Lab apart from any existing software solutions on the market.

References and useful resources

Websites

https://magento.com/
https://www.shopify.co.uk/tour/website-design
https://www.iwoca.co.uk/
https://www.thebabycotshop.com/
http://www.brandlabfashion.co.uk/

Part Five
Challenges for Bricks-and-Mortar Retailers

Understanding your lease – and how local authorities can benefit you

21

Key points

Understand your lease

The roles of government and local authorities

A brief overview of the Landlord and Tenant Act

The role and influence of the enlightened local authority

Understand your lease

A professional sky-diver would not jump unless every tiny detail of the parachute equipment had been checked before leaving the plane. As a professional retailer, you must take equal care before you sign a lease. It is essential you fully understand the contract you are committing your business to. We set out in this chapter sections of the Landlord and Tenant Act that you should be especially aware of and that we hope are changed in the future.

Some of these amendments you may well be able to negotiate with a landlord or a local authority who, in many cases, have taken over shop portfolios of landlords who have gone bankrupt. As we wrote in the introduction, start-ups are still needed, especially with the upheaval that the retail industry is experiencing. An abundance of growth opportunities across a diverse and innovative range of retail sectors in the UK and in international markets continues to exist. Retail consumers today focus on individual company propositions more than ever before and expect to access these retailers in many ways. Early stage retailers that integrate all the different methods of shopping, online and physical, that recognize the demands of today's consumer, will enjoy significant upside potential.

The roles of government and local authorities

Consumers and local communities can see what is going on in many towns across the UK – unattractive high streets dominated by empty spaces, charity shops, pound shops, building societies, banks, coffee shops, betting shops and, apart from food, very little else to encourage family shopping and entertainment. In many cases, they're no longer places in which to spend time and money. The balance or mix of shops that makes a shopping hub work is wrong in too many towns and smaller conurbations and the 'community' that continues to fail to get it are, sadly, landlords, local authorities and, most importantly, central government.

Unfortunately, the majority of mayors and civic leaders in the UK have so far failed to meet the current community challenge of making places more 'human' and reviving bricks-and-mortar retail. There are exceptions and later in this chapter we will highlight how two councils in the UK took the bull by the horns and turned round the fortunes of towns under their remit. We lobby for a reform to the Landlord and Tenant Act. The reason for this is to encourage new and exciting retailers to fill the spaces left by the complacent and inefficient traders who are now fast disappearing.

A brief overview of the Landlord and Tenant Act

In the UK, the Landlord and Tenant Act governs the rights and obligations of landlords and tenants of premises that are occupied for business purposes. In broad scope, the tenant of premises from which a business is carried on has security of tenure (means the right to stay) when the agreed term of their lease comes to an end, providing the tenant agrees to the asking rent at the time.

Below, we outline key elements of the Act that we believe should change to make the Act friendlier to tenants – and so they are the points you should be aware of and understand. There are links to both the 1954 and 1985 Acts in the References below.

Clearly a major rethink is needed for the high street. Multiples are struggling and opportunities are opening up for independents. If they are to survive, occupancy terms must be more favourable to allow them time to establish themselves. A more collaborative approach is vitally needed between landlord, tenant and council. Global Data, acting for American Express actually predict growth for the agile and reactive retail independent sector.

- Currently, at the end of the lease the landlord can ask for a rent that bears little relation to what the tenant is paying. The landlord uses evidence from other rental deals in the locality, often from newly arrived tenants who have very often been paid an incentive to open. This is called a reverse premium. When the existing tenant challenges this new level of rent, the landlord goes to a judging panel, called an arbitrator, whose decision binds both sides. In nearly every case, the arbitrator finds for the landlord and the existing tenant is forced out.

- What we want is security of tenure for the tenant at the end of lease and for the existing rent to be increased at the prevailing retail prices index (RPI), should the tenant wish to remain. This would be fair and give continuity to the community.

(*continued*)

(*Continued*)

- Currently, the main grounds for a landlord regaining possession of a property during the period of a lease would be if tenant defaults on rental payments or converts the property to a use not allowed in the lease. The Act as it stands now also allows the landlord to terminate the lease when it comes to an end by declaring a wish to rebuild the property in some form, without compensating the tenant. In many cases, the rebuilding is a device to terminate a lease in order to bring in a higher paying tenant.

- What we want, should the reason for termination be the rebuilding circumstances (assuming approved plans can be shown to the tenant), is for the tenant to be compensated with a payment equating to the past three years' rent. This will allow the tenant to find alternative premises and finance the move. If approved rebuilding plans cannot be shown six months prior to the end of the term, the lease will continue for a further three years at the prevailing rent. This change will make landlords think very carefully before terminating a lease without good cause.

- Currently, the arbitration process is very one-sided and nearly always finds for the landlord. It's also a legal and rather intimidating process for any business to negotiate. An arbitrator is called in if the landlord and tenant can't agree a rent when the lease ends.

- What we want, specifically for retail, is for the arbitration process to be fairer to both sides in the case of a dispute. If a rent cannot be agreed at lease end, the landlord needs to prove to the arbitrator that there are tenants lining up to take the space and be able to provide proof of new rental levels by giving three examples of shops of a similar size and in a similar location where rents exceed what the tenant has been paying. In that scenario, the existing tenant should either have the option to pay the new rent being demanded or, failing that, to receive a termination payment that equates to one year's rent.

- Currently, every lease has an upward-only rent review clause after five years and very few contain a tenant-only break clause.

- What we want is for every lease to have a tenant-only break clause after three years and six years. No lease should be longer than nine years and there should be RPI rental increases applied every year.

(*continued*)

(Continued)

- Currently, if a retail property is empty after three months the landlord pays 'empty shop rates' to the council. Many landlords prefer this to renting the shop at lower levels since this would mean an asset write-down that might mean a repayment to a bank or lender.

- What we want is that, if a retail property remains unoccupied for more than three months, the council can double empty shop rates and again by a third after nine months. This will encourage landlords to lower their rental expectations. If the property remains empty after six months, that landlord will be compelled to conduct an auction. The highest bidder will win occupation (two-year term) providing they can lodge, in advance, six months' rent. The local authority will manage the process.

Tip

We strongly recommend that you take professional advice when signing a lease or a licence; a lease is a complex contract.

The role and influence of the enlightened local authority

We've seen examples of how two local authorities in the UK were alarmed by the gradual deterioration of their high streets and the disloyal attitude of the local and effective shopping populations. An effective shopping population refers to consumers who travel in to a centre from a ten- to fifteen-mile radius and are the people who have a positive financial effect on the commerce in a town or city.

CASE STUDY Regenerating the Shropshire County Council market towns

Empty shops, unsafe after dark, shabby and tired streets, shoppers not returning, nothing for kids, poor nightlife, parking too expensive: where do you start?

Grey4Gold, run by Rowland Gee, completed the first consultation with Shropshire County Council in order to begin the revitalization of towns in the county. Rowland was struck by the council's determination to improve things on every level possible. The market towns were chosen as the revitalization pilot for developing a template to roll out to other distressed market towns throughout Shropshire.

The initial report focused on:

- current status of activities;
- where the town wants to be;
- how to get there.

Enquiries about vacant space came in and Grey4Gold, alongside the council, shortlisted the best candidates. Grey4Gold's ability to provide expert and professional business mentoring including inventory control, business planning, training programmes and design assistance along with retail assistance on merchandising and display, buying, identifying their market and marketing to their customer base to maximize revenues, were highly valued by the council. As part of the programme, Grey4Gold began visiting existing retailers to discuss ways to improve their stores and increase sales. This became an ongoing process. It is clear from the recommendations presented to the council that there has been an excellent start to a difficult problem that is being experienced throughout the country.

Probably one of the biggest problems facing towns today is the lack of 'joined-up' thinking between the council, the town steering groups, the local Chambers of Commerce, the police and local and regional tourism offices. Each of these entities works hard at seeking ways to reverse the decline of towns, but their functions would be far more powerful if they worked closer together to market the towns not only to their own community but also to a wider-based shopping population.

The Grey4Gold programme helped to bring minds and disjointed interests together and gradually vacancies dropped, incubator units were filled, traders improved their propositions, market days thrived and the towns began to recover.

Revitalizing a town is not just about filling space and painting storefronts. The biggest and most important issue is to bring the community along with the progress and make them a positive force for change within it.

Councils like Shropshire have tackled the key issues head on and have continued to work hard to maintain the big improvements they have made. They communicate what is being accomplished and show the community something is actually being done.

CASE STUDY Achieving retail success in Bicester town

The most successful outlet shopping centre in the world arrived in a quiet Oxfordshire town in the mid-1990s. It was called Bicester Village. The quiet adjacent town, Bicester, began to suffer. Was it because of the arrival of Bicester Village?

Actually, it was not; the decline was self-imposed. Very few local shoppers used the Village. The product there was expensive and appealed much more to UK tourists who liked shopping in central London, but were attracted because of everyday 30 per cent discounts. Bicester town suffered because the local traders, the council, the landlords, stopped talking to one another and simply blamed the Village. They overlooked the changes beginning to happen to UK retailing and refused to focus on customers' needs and aspirations.

A few years ago, when Rowland Gee first discussed the issues with Cherwell District Council (CDC), who wanted to arrest the decline in Bicester town centre, he presented a 15-point programme that included mentoring for independent retailers, engagement with landlords and detailed feedback sessions with consumers. Independent retailers and entrepreneurs have always sought outside influence and opinion for their businesses; they see it as an essential resource. The best mentors have the ability to guide and provoke ideas whilst respecting that they are dealing with the business owners' dreams and aspirations. CDC realized that quality mentoring goes well beyond just having an opinion and it's really hard to find.

In addition to that mentoring, Rowland shone a light on some rather unpleasant truths about how the town worked. The four most important bodies – the traders, the landlords, the consumers and the council – were simply not engaging. They all wanted the same thing: a thriving town. Rowland's influence, with the council's support, brought the parties together. The director of a national retail company, responsible for a large swathe of the town centre, had never actually visited

Bicester. Rowland had the ability to get him to the town and convinced him to take his responsibilities seriously as a major stakeholder in how the town operated. This director, with the support of the council, decided to let empty shops in the area under his control to new retailers and helped to relocate others. The council, to its credit, has continued the work. It has adopted Rowland's 15-point plan and, with a group of retailers coming together, things are improving.

There is still plenty of work to be done to make Bicester the town it deserves to be, but this example demonstrates clearly the power of resolve and clarity of intention.

What lessons can we learn from the positive actions of these councils?

The lessons we can draw from the proactive involvement of the Shropshire and Cherwell Councils is that first they appointed the equivalent of town centre managers and support teams who connected with landlords, consumers and shopkeepers. They listened hard to the issues Rowland Gee stated and drew up action plans to try to resolve them or at least make some positive headway. They concluded early on that for a town's shopping centre to be exciting it has to be compact. Gone were the days when shops could spread themselves over wide areas – far better to convert secondary and tertiary areas back into homes. The councils pledged to stay in touch with representatives of the three groups and continue the agreed reforms until they felt the towns were back on their feet. They quickly realized that if a town does not fulfil the expectations for all age groups, it fails. To meet ever more demanding expectations, they understood that a good variety of shops, low cost and flexible parking, great weekly food and local produce markets, weekend activities for the young, after-six dining and drinking facilities and other forms of entertainment were all services and attractions that must be delivered.

A lively town manager will do all sorts of things to bring life back. In Market Drayton in Shropshire, a disused church became a community centre where people of all ages congregate to hold events, to show first-run movies, to hold kids' parties, to play bridge, or just have a coffee and so much more. Market Drayton transformed an old town centre storage area into an incubator centre for retail pop-ups, many of which later took permanent shops after they discovered they had a winner on their hands. You could feel the buzz in the town and success bred success. The market expanded from 50 metres in length to 500 metres with specialty stalls selling varieties of treacle, fudges, jams and honeys, breads, wines, meats and eggs, all locally produced and farmed. That's what an enlightened council can do and there are over 350 councils in the UK.

And then there's the history. So many places have an interesting historical past and there is nothing kids love more than dressing up in Roman costumes, holding swords and marching through the town. This strategy that some have adopted has brought kids back to town at weekends and will halt the leakage of families to bigger conurbations. Too many councils have sat back and not applied a unique or bespoke approach to revive their towns and this is especially sad in the UK, since half the population live in these great places. No one wants to live in a failing town.

As a start-up, be sure that, if you do decide to open a shop in a medium-sized or small town, meet first with the council and be sure they are delivering or are determined to deliver the components and improvements we have described in these two case studies. If you're not sure, or don't sense the passion, you can walk away. They need you.

References and useful resources

Further reading

Davidson, R (1 June 2017) 'Commercial leases: a guide to the Landlord and Tenant Act 1954', Burnetts Blog [online]. Available at: https://www. burnetts.co.uk/publications/blogs/commercial-leases-a-guide-to-the-landlord-and-tenant-act-1954

Useful resources

https://www.globaldata.com/

Landlord and Tenant Act 1954 [online]. Available at: http://www.legis lation.gov.uk/ukpga/Eliz2/2-3/56/contents

Landlord and Tenant Act 1985 [online]. Available at: https://www.legis lation.gov.uk/ukpga/1985/70

Part Six
How Good Should Become Sensational

Why good today is not good enough in the current retail trade

22

Key points

Be inspired by the greats

Apply the vital four Ms

Check your business's health

Never lose your excitement and always trust yourself

Sensational retailers

Be amazing or die. This may sound dramatic, but the bricks-and-mortar retail sector has been squeezed – between consumer belt-tightening, high rents, business rates and the huge growth in online shopping. But, as we said in the introduction of this book, the retail 'cake' has not shrunk. In Chapter 1, we outlined key statistics that clearly demonstrates consumers are continuing to spend (in fact, they're spending more); it's where consumers are spending and what motivates them to spend that has dramatically changed in the last decade.

The massive rise of online shopping that has been embraced by shoppers worldwide has had obvious repercussions on shops and stores, but what many shopkeepers have not taken on board is that consumers, when shopping online, make very fast decisions. They draw positive or negative impressions from factors such as the greeting, the product, the selection, the style, the ease of identification, the quality, the price and information, the payment processes and the shipping and returns policies. These impressions and assumptions now carry over into the high street shopper's mentality and if a trader's proposition does not hit home fast, the moment will have gone. That is today's challenge for retail businesses, and we will illustrate in this chapter examples of retailers, large and small, that have wholeheartedly embraced this change of mentality and expectation amongst consumers and are now sensational.

CASE STUDY   Marvin Traub

The late Marvin Traub, one of retailing's greatest showmen and innovators, had his view of the future. He met Rowland Gee in 2008, just prior to the publication of his book *Like No Other Career*. 'The retailer of the future,' he writes in the book, 'will be a true multichannel player, one that enhances the traditional department store with an expanded retail presence including a catalogue, a website, and perhaps the addition of home shopping. The consumer will be able to shop at his or her favourite store anytime and through a variety of shopping techniques. The successful retailer of the future will still have to focus on creating an image and excitement across all channels. Technology is simply an asset for doing that. Ultimately, however, it all begins with the product. The big winners in 21st-century retailing will be those stores that fully take advantage of our ever-changing technology and combine it with great merchandising.' Traub was a legendary shopkeeper and those predictive words written in 2008 have come true, big time. It was Traub who, while running Bloomingdale's in New York from 1978 to 1992, persuaded the world's greatest brands (and some he believed would become great brands) to open corners in Bloomingdale's. This was new – up till then brands were just placed around the store on rails and on shelves. Traub brought the Marshall McLuhan phrase 'The medium is the message' to life. By persuading brands like Giorgio Armani, Gucci, Christian Dior,

Chanel and others to open in Bloomingdale's, in sumptuous corners, he propelled Bloomingdale's to the very top of the international department store ladder. Others followed around the world, but Traub never lost his iconic place amongst the innovators and disrupters. 'Will there be more great merchants?' Gee asked Traub. 'There are always opportunities in retailing,' he said. 'Who finds them and who seizes upon them will be the ongoing challenge and will produce the great merchants of 2040.'

Who are these great merchants today and how have they travelled from just being good to sensational? To begin with, their message is clear; the merchandise is brilliantly selected and displayed; the meeting and greeting, whether instore or online, is welcoming and professional; and the marketing of the operation, social media, website advertising and instore window displays are all spot on. Now we'll look at some examples.

Sensational retailers today

- Selfridges
- Goyard
- Borough Market
- Museum shops
- Bicester Village

Selfridges

Selfridges can't be a niche store – it's too big – but it can nevertheless confidently retain its outlook and spread its personality and ethos over every single department it operates. Customers from teenagers to seniors love the store because it responds to their tastes without destroying their respective aspirations and emotions. This really is very hard to pull off, but Selfridges has achieved this by never patronizing the different age groups and by making them all feel special with facilities and atmospheres, audible and visual, that make them feel great.

As Marvin Traub predicted, those who seek success will have to create an image and excitement across all channels. Selfridges is a brilliant example of excellence because it has never stood still. It engages with its customers before it upgrades departments and has launched a Chinese-language website to support that growing market. A visit has become an experience in every sense of the word. In late 2018, it opened an Art Deco-themed brasserie that will have its own street access. The centrepiece will be a huge crystal-encrusted mythical figure of Pegasus, designed by Damien Hirst. Restaurateurs like Richard Caring, who runs an exclusive chain of restaurants, would never have considered opening in a department store ten years ago, but such has been the achievement of the brilliant repositioning of Selfridges that he never gave it a second thought. As Caring said recently to Jonathan Prynn, Consumer Business Editor, *London Evening Standard* on 4 October 2018, 'When you think of the capital city of the world, you think of London and when you think of London, you think of Selfridges.'

We strongly recommend you take a long, slow walk around this store to fully absorb the minutiae and detail that goes into making a store world-class and then review its website to see how this approach follows through.

Goyard

Goyard, a luggage, leather goods and accessories company, describes itself as a trunkmaker. It began life as a retail start-up in Paris in 1853 and the original shop in Rue Saint Honoré still remains, beautifully preserved in all its glory. Goyard's strategy has been to remain a private company, never to advertise in traditional media, but to embrace Instagram with beautifully photographed and moving images. They have 19 shops worldwide where all the business is done. Goyard's clientele includes some very famous names, from Picasso to Beyoncé, who cherished and continue to cherish the subtlety and elegance of the products. Goyard has never strayed from its core beliefs and still uses, on all products, its famous 'badge of rank' – a chevron design with a tiny and subtle Goyard-Honoré embedded within it. Its appeal is that it has never strayed from its original brand outlook, has only used the finest materials and always produced its products using the finest artisanal methods. Goyard has survived because it has listened and responded to its customers' lifestyle demands, while never compromising its quality, style or brand identity.

What we take from this story is how a brand can sustain itself by sticking to its exclusive principles, never getting drawn into areas it knows little about and never over-expanding. What, however, Goyard *has* demonstrated in its 165-year journey is that it is prepared to embrace new technology. It has moved from hand-painted products to printing and the high-tech materials it uses for non-leather products are very much 21st-century developments. Goyard recognizes customers' love for personalization and will hand-paint a customer's initials on to its products. It will produce bespoke trunks. We love the fact that its personal service ethos is demonstrated by never allowing clients into a shop unless they can receive one-to-one service. Even in today's impatient world people will be patient if they know what they want to buy is indeed special. That is what we call sensational.

Borough Market

How can a 1,000-year-old market be described as sensational? Well, simply put, everything on sale in Borough Market, every type of produce from Alsop & Walker's cheeses and eggs, to Field & Flower's raw honeys to Wiltshire Chilli Farm's chilli-based sauces and Wright Brothers incredible shellfish, is all sensationally good and all products can be traced back to source. Every one of the hundreds of traders there share the identical mission: to provide the customer with the very best and give them the service to go with it. To retain its place amongst the top five food markets in the world (others being Budapest's Central Market Hall, Sydney Fish Market, Seattle's Pike Place Market and Berlin's Markthalle Neun) speaks volumes about the standards Borough Market has retained and how the open-minded attitude of studying these markets continues to raise standards. Borough Market is a co-operative in the sense that it fosters positive internal peer pressure where no one wants to let the show down and it continues to demonstrate willingness to concentrate and learn from these other great markets. It's truly impressive.

We draw several lessons from Borough Market that your start-up can benefit from: specialize in a product you feel comfortable in dealing with, retain an open and curious mind, be prepared to give great service, and if produce becomes your area of choice never ever compromise on quality.

Museum shops

Andy Warhol once predicted that most department stores will become museums and all museums will become department stores. He was ahead of his time. All across the world, museums have upped their game. Today, when we visit a museum (and millions more are each year), we exit through a shop. We visit the museums because the exhibitions they mount are thought-provoking, terrifically curated and wonderfully lit. The exhibitions are concentrated on specific topics and the museums realize that visitors won't come through the door if it simply offers a walk through endless rooms of stuff. So, like today's best retail operations, museums understand the principle of focus and demographic targeting. They also understand that when the visitor exits the show, the shop can't be a let-down.

Many museum shops don't disappoint – in fact, they can be brilliant gift stores and many people now do their birthday and Christmas shopping in one. Why are they so good? The teams that run the best museums talk to each other and communicate the techniques they will use and the aesthetic that they will adopt, and hope to achieve, for any particular event. Next time you go to an exhibit, feel the atmosphere as you enter, look around and spot the many forms of lighting techniques and equipment installed to bring the exhibits to life, look at the use of digital media, focus on the dramatic staging and the descriptive panels of information. This is the highest form of retailing because it's about intoxicating you with the intention of bowling you over. When you move into the retail shop it has to live up to that emotion – and they do.

These shops are often wonderfully curated with items that cleverly link to what you have seen and then go beyond. Great shelving sees products lit individually, with the most up-to-date racking and shelving techniques designed specifically for the products they display. Very efficient checkout points often include a great wrapping service. In London, we love the V&A, the Tate Modern, the Design Museum and the British Museum; in New York, the Guggenheim and MOMA; in Paris, the Louvre; and in Vienna, the Kunsthistorisches Museum. There are many more, of course, but the point we want to stress is that these institutions are moving in lock step because they realize they have exploited a gap in the retail market.

As a start-up, perhaps with a view to gift retailing, you can gather tremendously useful information for your upcoming operation from examining carefully and researching these operations. Remember, too, that retailing does not stop at the museum itself – the online sites are a knockout as well and absolutely consistent with the physical experience. If you ever want to buy a Warhol print today, and many do, where do you go? You visit a museum shop.

Bicester Village

Bicester Village in Oxfordshire, UK is part of Value Retail, an 11-outlet Village shopping group positioned across the world. All the tenants or brands are on one-year leases. Each pays a percentage of sales, but none pays a fixed rent. Each outlet Village has an organization of six merchants or controllers who work with the tenants to make them successful. The standards imposed are rigorous and demanding, but the retail results are astounding. There are few greater success stories in fashion than Value Retail and its crowning glory is Bicester Village, which is almost certainly the highest performing shopping destination in terms of sales per square metre anywhere in the world.

The Village has created specific training modules for its people that combine retail with hospitality as part of a prerequisite to work there. The ethos of the Village is that 'salespeople' should not think of themselves as salespeople, but as butlers and concierges. The simple formula is that if a store is not successful Value Retail does not renew the lease.

There is a waiting list of people who would like to join the centre that truly creates a partnership between the developer and the retailer. They work together to achieve great productivity. In any given year, about 15 per cent of the tenants move, either to larger spaces, smaller spaces, or out altogether. Everyone buys into this eco system and standards are sky high. These standards include fresh flower displays, spotlessly clean walkways, toilets, car parks and general open areas. You won't see a chewing gum spot anywhere. What is so impressive about this relentless attention to detail is that everyone responds. The brands, the people who run the shops, the shoppers and the Village have all come together to create an atmosphere of sheer excellence. We talked about peer pressure in Borough Market and it's evident here too. If a window display is grubby or tired, if a doormat is worn, if a light is out in a store, if a shelf is left bare, if a flower display has drooped, if there are no towels or loo paper in the lavatories, then it's noticed and attended to, quickly. That's what we mean by team effort: single-minded focus. And guess what? The consumer responds. It is a sensational and ground-breaking organization.

How you can become sensational

What connects these great retailers, establishments and organizations is that they all set about to establish themselves as leaders and influencers within their respective fields. How have they all travelled from just being good to sensational? To begin with, they all had a plan and a strategy and stuck with it. Their messages are clear; the merchandise is brilliantly focused, selected and displayed; the meeting and greeting, whether in a premises or online, is welcoming and professional; and the marketing of the operations, including advertising, social media, website, customer connections and in store window display, is outstanding. We refer to these dynamics as the four Ms.

The Four Ms

- **Message**: Always be clear and focused, through windows, interiors, product and making the proposition clear.

- **Merchandising**: Concentrate on products being segmented and understandable. Content is everything and product selection must be well-sourced, curated and displayed.

- **Meeting and greeting**: Offer warm and informative service, giving an outstanding experience, both instore and online.

- **Marketing**: It's vital to maintain consistency, hold regular events, develop loyalty programmes, involve social media, and of course build a knockout website. Create a marketing calendar to remain in touch with your database. Know and understand your competitors and always remember the power of being a team, both inside and outside the business, including suppliers, landlords and local councils.

Really look at yourself and take a 'health check'

A. The market, your strategy and testing your vision

- What retail segment do you fit into?
- How large (value) is your market?
- Has your market grown or declined in the last five years?
- Who are the biggest players?
- What percentage do they hold?
- What's left for the independents?
- Who are your nearest competitors?
- Has footfall grown or declined in your area?
- What are the population trends in your area?
- If population has declined, where has it gone?
- Your landlord and your relationship.
- What do you want to be?
- Develop and refine your business plan.
- Monitor the execution of tactics and strategy.

B. Financial, operations and performance

- Do you have a 'trusted' stock control system?
- If you don't, do you know how to get one?
- If you do, what structure do you have in place to analyse the data?
- Do you know how to calculate margin and do you have a net margin objective?
- Do you have a stock turn objective?
- Do you have a stock profile objective?
- What are your buying and decision-making processes?
- Do you have a sourcing strategy?
- Do you buy from agents or direct from source?
- Do you do monthly P&L accounts?
- Do you have a cash flow analysis and forecast?
- Do you run a WSSI (weekly sales and stock intake plan)?
- Do you know your ATV (average transaction value)?
- Do you track your footfall conversion? (actual vs target).
- Agree the key performance indicators (KPIs).
- Never allow your systems (manual or IT) to let you down.

C. How to stand out in a crowded market

- Is your offer clearly defined and presented?
- Is your offer functional or aspirational?
- Do your customers quickly understand your offer?
- Does your business visually and physically communicate clarity of proposition?
- Do your staff communicate the ethos of the store?
- Do you work at your supplier relationships?
- The first and last impressions your customers get have to be good, every time.
- Be a know-all: know your market and know your customer.

D. Learning about your business, setting and measuring goals

- Do you regularly get to know what your customers think of you?
- Do you regularly involve your staff regarding customer feedback?
- Do you ask your staff what they think of the relevance of your proposition and how it could improve?
- Do you (internally) hold a twice-yearly SWOT analysis. Who takes part?
- Do you train/appraise your staff and measure their performance?
- Who does what in your business?
- Accountability and responsibility for functions.

E. E-tailing, social media & multi-channel

The importance of differentiation in an increasingly competitive market

- Occupy a marketplace that sidesteps having to compete on price: avoid 'fatal' price wars.
- Provide a high-quality shopping experience and a clear proposition.
- Build and develop loyalty with your customers by adding complementary benefits.

Operations, customer analysis and communication

- SEO
- Make browsing easy.
- Make the checkout process easy.
- Understand the importance of social media.
- Customer interaction.

Monitoring and reacting

- Visits: day/week/month/average.
- New visits.
- Repeat visits.
- Conversion percentage.
- Traffic sources.
- Feedback strategy.

Choice, convenience and growth

- Are you constantly refreshing and updating your choice, and is your choice always consistent with your stated market position?
- Are you thinking about the next step?
- If you operate a bricks-and-mortar store, how do you cross market?

References and useful resources

References

Borough Market (28 Sept 2018) 'Borough Market welcomes new chair of trustees' [online]. Available at: http://boroughmarket.org.uk/articles/borough-market-welcomes-new-chair-of-trustees

Traub, M (2008) *Like No Other Career*, Assouline Publishing, New York

Websites

https://www.thebicestervillageshoppingcollection.com/en/value-retail/
http://boroughmarket.org.uk/
https://www.britishmuseumshoponline.org/
https://designmuseumshop.com/
https://www.farfetch.com
https://www.goyard.com/en
https://www.museumoficecream.com/
http://www.selfridges.com
https://shop.tate.org.uk/
https://www.vam.ac.uk/shop/

Useful resources

Get Started Selling on Amazon: https://services.amazon.co.uk/?ld=SEUKSOAAD Gog-Branded-WMT_amazon-market-places_p_205904435180_c
https://www.pinterest.co.uk/foyjw/visual-merchandising/
https://www.pinterest.co.uk/martinorme/cool-shops-london/

Conclusion

Your journey

Throughout this book, we have outlined the steps you should take in setting up a retail business and underlined how important it is to carry out due diligence in each key area we have identified in the book's various sections. It is vital to have an understanding of these processes before you embark on your start-up journey.

1 Create the vision.

2 Work out your best routes to market.

3 Demonstrate, to yourself and others, how best to compete.

4 Market and communicate effectively to customers, suppliers, landlords, local authorities, banks and potential investors.

5 Set up the business controls so you know what's going on.

6 Manage your money.

Being prepared to enter the retail arena, regardless of the confidence you have in your idea, will be worth your time. You wouldn't jump into a car and drive off unless you passed the driving test. Or you might, but you could have an accident, you would certainly fall out with the authorities, and you could even harm your nearest and dearest. Consider that example and take the time, probably three to four months, to do your homework. It will increase your confidence and you will be truly informed and knowledgeable. Add all that to your vision and you will have assembled a pretty impressive manifesto. This background knowledge and being able to speak of it will come in handy when convincing customers and all the people and organizations you will meet as you begin your journey.

Opportunities for you are increasing all the time. Retail property investors are facing up to a drop in values that are leading through to lower rents and new housing developments are bringing consumers with them. The government in the UK is, at last, responding. Business rates will be cut for small shops and local authorities are being challenged to bring back residents to town centres, to create more of a community feeling in towns by widening the retail offering and thus the town's general appeal. A good example of this is in the town of Bicester in Oxfordshire, a town we highlighted in the previous chapter. Many vibrant independent shops and businesses have sprung up following the council's determination to grasp the nettle. Tim & David's coffee shop in the Market Square has the smoothest lattes you can imagine; Emma the florist produces bouquets of stunning beauty; Sarah's gift shop always smells just the best; Richard and his family, the stationers, help all businesses to get the job done. Nia & James's furniture shop up by the church is one of Bicester's hidden gems as is Ian's antique shop and the wonderful Coles bookshop that sells an amazing collection of signed first editions – and does it brilliantly online, too. Julian and Sara's print shop and Jane's boutique, chic and unique in equal measure, have – together with all the others – brought the enterprise and created the variety the town so badly needed. The product is right, customers are responding.

Retail's new generation

In retail terms, the opposite of crisis is opportunity. The King's Cross area in London that, only a decade ago, was a dirty, dangerous, run-down and grubby part of London is witnessing new life. Who would have thought that a huge Google office, a nine-floor Facebook office coming soon, Central Saint Martins College of Art and Design, and great new restaurants and bars would spring up on reclaimed land and bring fresh and exciting life to the area. Behind the railway station, there are arches first used as coal yards in the 19th century and then for haulage in the 1950s. These spaces will soon be reopened as Coal Drops Yard and fitted out for retail spaces. Famous names such as Paul Smith, Wolf & Badger and Tom Dixon will trade alongside innovative start-ups of every retail complexion. This development proves conclusively that enterprise and imagination will win through, so prepare yourself well and become part of retail's new generation.

We warned in the introduction to this book that retail is not an easy ride. What you have to do from the outset is trust in yourself and your vision. You have to listen to people, and take their counsel, but always trust in yourself. You are the person with the vision, you are the person who needs to sell your ideas to many people and take them on a journey with you. You are the person who will make the enterprise a reality.

We have set out in this book many examples of real people with real stories, who have worked hard to achieve lasting success. We have carefully selected these examples – it was not always an easy ride for them and they have had to show tremendous tenacity and endurance.

No story exemplifies this more than a company called Everything Branded. Paul Rowlett, an Iraq war veteran, founded the company more than seven years ago. Rowlett was a Navy man and after coming home he lost everything when his home was repossessed. He and his wife were living on benefits. After attending conferences and being gifted 'goody' bags, Rowlett had an idea. He decided to produce promotional products, including items such as key rings, mugs, notebooks, pens, mints, polo shirts – in fact, any item that could bear the logo or brand of the company holding an event. Business began slowly, but after he approached Leicester Council in the UK and suggested he produce mugs to celebrate the Queen's Diamond Jubilee and give them away free to the council, this generous gesture was noticed and Everything Branded took off. The company now employs over 100 people, designing and offering a vast range of merchandise. Business is great.

What we have also stressed in this book is the importance of the research needed to back up your trading choice, the installation of simple controls and setting up regular operational disciplines, and putting everything in the diary. Don't be put off this 'back of house' work. You will be happy that you spent time, right at the beginning, installing the measures we suggest in this book. Recall what we pointed out about meeting with banks and investors: they will run a mile if you can't back up your vision with a plan that is well thought through and clearly set out.

Retailers today have to be more imaginative than ever before, but must also never lose sight of the big picture. They have to think, all the time, about the various parts of their enterprise. A holistic approach is essential and that's why we continually return to the fact that you need to become a 'know all' for your business.

As we said in the introduction, being a good retailer is not good enough today. Being exceptional or even sensational must be your target and you should be prepared to be hardworking, focused and dedicated to delivering your vision. It takes a special kind of dedication and unwavering tenacity to make it work.

Starting a business today is an opportunity, and there really is a need for new blood. We hope this book will become your go-to handbook, which you can regularly refer to for guidance, use to ensure you are never overlooking key issues, and that will help you to deal with unexpected challenges that will inevitably come up.

Retail is a great career as it gives you the opportunity to buy, sell, plan and motivate. It's particularly rewarding because not only will it give you gratification when you experience positive reactions to your choices, but it provides direct interaction with your customers that will enable you to react, gather feedback, move forward and develop your vision. Get yourself fit for purpose and the only way is up.

References and useful resources

https://www.everythingbranded.co.uk/

GLOSSARY

Cash flow: The amount of cash and cash equivalents entering and leaving the business.

Cost price: The price you pay to produce the goods and services you are selling.

Fixed assets: A long-term tangible piece of property the company owns (eg capital expenditure).

Fixed costs: (also referred to as fixed overheads) Costs, such as rent, rates and utility bills, that will not change with a fluctuation in sales.

Gross profit: (also referred to as gross income and gross margin) Amount left from the sales revenues, less VAT if applicable, after deducting the cost of sales (anything you have to buy to produce the goods and services you are selling).

Net margin: The margin, after VAT and cost of sales have been deducted from gross sales.

Net profit: (before corporation tax) The amount left after the fixed and variable overheads have been deducted from the gross profit.

Profit and loss account: Profit and loss account summarizes the revenue/income and the costs/expenses/overheads during a specific period of time.

SPTE: Selling price tax exclusive

SPTI: Selling price tax inclusive

Stock turns (also referred to as stock turnover or inventory turnover): The number of times you have sold/replaced your stock in a time period, such as a year. To obtain the stock turn ratio, divide the cost of sales by the average stock.

Variable costs: (also referred to as variable overheads) Costs that vary with sales, such as raw materials, salaries/wages.

VAT: Value Added Tax

APPENDIX

Explanatory notes for the example of different gross profit margin calculations

Part 1

Retail selling price including VAT (A) minus VAT @ 16.67% = Retail selling price excluding VAT (B)

Retail selling price excluding VAT (B) minus Cost price (C) = Gross profit margin (D)

Retail selling price excluding VAT (B) ÷ 100 times Gross profit margin % (E) = Gross profit margin (D)

Part 2

To calculate retail selling price excluding VAT:

VAT (A) ÷ 100, times Gross profit margin % (B) = Gross profit margin (C)

To arrive at 20 per cent for VAT (UK) where a product has been sold inclusive of VAT, use one of the following two methods of calculation. For example, a jacket at £50 inclusive of VAT:

£50 ÷ 100 x 16.67 = £8.33 (20% VAT)
OR: £50 ÷ 1.2 = £41.67 - £50 = £8.33 (20% VAT)

To prove that £8.33 is the correct VAT amount for that particular product, check it another way. We know that the selling price for the jacket without VAT is £41.67: £41.67 ÷ 100 x 20 = £8.33 or £50.00 ÷ 1.2 = £41.67 deducted from £50.00 = £8.33

INDEX